LIBRARY MANUALS

Volume 11

A MANUAL OF CHILDREN'S LIBRARIES

A MANUAL OF CHILDREN'S LIBRARIES

W.C. BERWICK SAYERS

LONDON AND NEW YORK

First published in 1932 by George Allen & Unwin Ltd
This edition first published in 2022
by Routledge
4 Park Square, Milton Park, Abingdon, Oxon OX14 4RN

and by Routledge
605 Third Avenue, New York, NY 10017

Routledge is an imprint of the Taylor & Francis Group, an informa business

Copyright © 1932 by Taylor & Francis.

All rights reserved. No part of this book may be reprinted or reproduced or utilised in any form or by any electronic, mechanical, or other means, now known or hereafter invented, including photocopying and recording, or in any information storage or retrieval system, without permission in writing from the publishers.

Trademark notice: Product or corporate names may be trademarks or registered trademarks, and are used only for identification and explanation without intent to infringe.

British Library Cataloguing in Publication Data
A catalogue record for this book is available from the British Library

ISBN: 978-1-03-213109-2 (Set)
ISBN: 978-1-00-322771-7 (Set) (ebk)
ISBN: 978-1-03-213592-2 (Volume 11) (hbk)
ISBN: 978-1-03-213596-0 (Volume 11) (pbk)
ISBN: 978-1-00-323002-1 (Volume 11) (ebk)

DOI: 10.4324/9781003230021

Publisher's Note
The publisher has gone to great lengths to ensure the quality of this reprint but points out that some imperfections in the original copies may be apparent.

Disclaimer
The publisher has made every effort to trace copyright holders and would welcome correspondence from those they have been unable to trace.

A MANUAL OF CHILDREN'S LIBRARIES

by

W. C. BERWICK SAYERS

CHIEF LIBRARIAN OF THE CROYDON
PUBLIC LIBRARIES

Author of "An Introduction to Classification," "A Manual of Classification," etc.

LONDON
GEORGE ALLEN & UNWIN LTD
AND THE LIBRARY ASSOCIATION
1932

FIRST PUBLISHED IN 1932

All rights reserved
PRINTED IN GREAT BRITAIN BY
UNWIN BROTHERS LTD., WOKING

GENERAL INTRODUCTION TO THE SERIES

The publication of a systematic series of practical and authoritative Manuals of Library Work, which shall survey Library polity and practice in their latest aspects, is a requirement of which administrators, librarians, and students alike have long been conscious, and is much overdue.

In the Library world not the Great War alone, with its aftermath of new conditions, but also the Library Act of 1919, have marked the termination of one long epoch and the commencement of a new and yet more prosperous era. The removal of the crippling limitation of the penny rate at once paved the way for a renaissance of the Library Movement, and remarkable extensions and innovations, both in buildings and in service, have ensued. The great work of the Carnegie Trustees in fostering the development of urban Public Libraries has been largely diverted into fresh channels, and County and Rural Library Systems now cover the country from Land's End to John-o'-Groats. The public demand and appreciation of Libraries have increased enormously, and, in response, old methods have been revised and new ones introduced. The evolution of Commercial and Technical Libraries and the development of Business and Works Libraries would amply suffice to indicate this spirit of progress, but, during the last decade or so, the entire field of

A MANUAL OF CHILDREN'S LIBRARIES

Library service has been subjected to review and experiment, and little, either in administration or routine, remains entirely unchanged.

It will, therefore, be sufficiently obvious that the old text books relating to Library practice can no longer serve, and that there is a real need for new manuals, written by persons of experience and authority, and treating of the new conditions in a full and thoroughly practical manner. It is this void that the series of Library Manuals is designed to fill, and the fact that these volumes are to be issued by Messrs. George Allen and Unwin Ltd. in conjunction with the Library Association, should afford adequate proof of the qualifications of the authors to treat of the subjects upon which they will write. If sufficient support is forthcoming the series will be made comprehensive and complete.

The volumes will be supplied with bibliographical references throughout, and will be illustrated where necessary. No effort will be spared to make the series an essential tool for all those who are engaged in Library work, or who intend to embrace Librarianship as a profession. To students they will be invaluable. The uniform price of 10s. 6d. net will be adhered to so far as possible, so as to bring the Manuals within the reach of all.

Wm. E. DOUBLEDAY
General Editor

PREFACE

Some years ago I published a little book called *The Children's Library*, which has long been out of print. In it I dealt with the methods used and proposed by librarians and others for the provision for and the exploiting of the reading propensities of the young. It was a book written in the light of the experience of American rather than that of English librarians. In America it has been recognized for the past forty years that if the adult is to be a trained, or an economical user of books—that is to say, if he is to use them with knowledge and with the capacity to extract the best from them—he must be trained in their use; and in all towns of consequence children's departments in the public libraries have been provided out of the public funds, and administered with a liberality almost unbelievable in any other country. In England, tentative efforts, some of them very successful, had been made from about 1855 onwards, to do something on similar if much more modest lines, but only in the years since the Great War has any sort of opportunity of supplying it come to this country. In 1917 the Library Association passed this resolution which I think it is not unfair to say marked an epoch in this matter, since it set all the progressive librarians in this country thinking anew upon the matter:—

The creation in the child of intellectual interests, which is furthered by a love of books, is an urgent national need;

A MANUAL OF CHILDREN'S LIBRARIES

while it is the business of this School to foster the desire to know, it is the business of the library to give adequate opportunity for the satisfaction of this desire; library work with children ought to be the basis of all other library work; reading rooms should be provided in all public libraries, where children may read books in attractive surroundings, with the sympathetic and tactful help of trained children's librarians; but such provision will be largely futile except under the conditions which experience has shown to be essential to success.

To this end all librarians are now working; and the things I wrote of in *The Children's Library* as hopeful possibilities are now in many cases actualities.

The present work is one of a series of handbooks of librarianship, and that implies that its first appeal is to the professed student of librarianship. While this is so, I have tried to make the book of more general interest. Every book-lover is to some extent an amateur librarian, and those who have to supervise or provide for the reading of children embrace a very large number of people. I have, therefore, tried to be helpful in such matters as the selection and preservation of children's books, which matters concern almost all adults, and to furnish simple guidance for teachers, and Sunday school teacher-librarians in the details which experience shows to lead to the best use of libraries.

I have built on the work of almost everyone who has written upon this subject; but I have kept to my own observation and experience very largely; and those of my colleagues who favour me with a glance at this book are begged to believe that I have

PREFACE

tried to describe such of their methods as I know impartially in the light of my own experience in the directing of children's libraries. I have endeavoured to keep within what is practicable for a well-organized British library system with only moderate funds and a small staff. The difficulty lies largely in this staff question; until it is realized that the children require separate handling by librarians specially adapted in personality and prepared by careful training, successful public libraries for children are impossible. I hope this book will do something to further this important matter.

Bearing in mind the objects of this series, I have added to each chapter a list of the books which I think will be most useful to the student. The subject is written, and over-written, to an extent which is bewildering—a confession which the writer of another book on it may make with penitence—and there are bibliographies of really amazing length in Sophy H. Powell's *The Children's Library* (116 pages), and Gwendolen Rees's *Libraries for Children* (56 pages). The magazine articles listed in Cannons's *Bibliography of Library Economy*, 1876–1920, run to 72 double-columned pages and about four thousand entries, and that was the state of things eleven years ago. I have thought that a *selection* of references will serve a useful purpose.

The many things I have written about have been worked out by a devoted children's staff in the Croydon libraries. To Miss Ethel G. Hayler and the library force working with her I owe much for the creative way in which they have worked for our children; ordinary hours and duties have been exceeded so often that such sacrifices have been in danger of becoming almost commonplace; and their initiative has been most fruitful.

I acknowledge with thanks the loan from my brother librarians of several of the illustrations which adorn this book. To Miss L. Margaret Haley I am indebted for much help.

W. C. BERWICK SAYERS

CONTENTS

CHAPTER		PAGE
	PREFACE	9
	LIST OF ILLUSTRATIONS	15

PART I.—THE BOOK

I.	CHILDREN'S BOOKS OF THE PAST	19
II.	WHAT CHILDREN READ TO-DAY	34
III.	THE BOOK AS CRAFTSMANSHIP	55
IV.	BOOK SELECTION AND ACCESSION	63
V.	THE CARE OF BOOKS	74
VI.	BOOKBINDING	87

PART II.—THE CHILDREN'S LIBRARY

VII.	MAKING THE CHILDREN'S LIBRARY	97
VIII.	THE EQUIPMENT OF THE LIBRARY	112
IX.	THE ARRANGEMENT OF BOOKS	125
X.	THE CATALOGUE AND HOW TO MAKE IT	148

PART III.—THE LIBRARIAN'S WORK

XI.	THE LIBRARIAN AND THE WORK OF THE LIBRARY	165
XII.	TEACHING THE USE OF THE LIBRARY	180

A MANUAL OF CHILDREN'S LIBRARIES

CHAPTER		PAGE
XIII.	LECTURES	192
XIV.	THE STORY HOUR	207
XV.	READINGS, DRAMATIC READINGS AND PLAYER CLUBS	213
XVI.	EXHIBITIONS, ILLUSTRATION COLLECTIONS	218
XVII.	PUBLICITY AND PUBLICATIONS AND THE RELATIONSHIPS OF THE LIBRARY	223
XVIII.	SCHOOL LIBRARIES—GENERAL	230
XIX.	SCHOOL LIBRARIES—MUNICIPAL	238

EPILOGUE

XX.	A WORD WITH THE CHILDREN'S LIBRARIAN	253
	APPENDIX—SOME EXAMINATION QUESTIONS	259
	INDEX	267

ILLUSTRATIONS

IN THE CHILDREN'S LIBRARY
    From a painting by Lucy Baker
        Lent by the Woolwich Public Libraries
	Frontispiece

	FACING PAGE
NO. 1 JOY STREET, LIVERPOOL *Lent by the Liverpool Public Libraries*	40
SHOWING HOW TO OPEN A LIBRARY BOOK	80
PLANS OF CHILDREN'S LIBRARIES Drawn by Eva K. West	96

I   { 1. In a room divided only by furniture
      2. With a separate department for the Lending Library
      3. With a glazed barrier dividing Lending and Reading Departments	

PLANS OF CHILDREN'S LIBRARIES Drawn by Eva K. West	104

II   { 4. With all activities in one square room
      5. With a special room for reference work and Story-Telling
      6. In a very busy area, with separate Reference and Story-Telling Rooms	

THE HUNSLET JUNIOR LIBRARY, LEEDS *Photograph lent by the Leeds Public Libraries*	112
THE NORBURY CHILDREN'S LIBRARY, CROYDON	120
A SHEAF CATALOGUE *Courtesy of Libraco Ltd.*	152
A SHEAF CATALOGUE OPEN TO SHOW METHOD OF CONSULTATION *Courtesy of Libraco Ltd.*	152

A MANUAL OF CHILDREN'S LIBRARIES

	FACING PAGE
A Card Catalogue Cabinet *Courtesy of Libraco Ltd.*	156
Drawer of a Card Catalogue *Courtesy of Libraco Ltd.*	160
One-Drawer Card Catalogue, showing Construction *Courtesy of Libraco Ltd.*	160
The Story Hour at the Ashburton Library, Croydon	208
Mounting Illustrations	220

PART I
THE BOOK

IN THE CHILDREN'S LIBRARY
From a painting by Lucy Baker. Lent by the Woolwich Public Libraries

CHAPTER I

CHILDREN'S BOOKS
OF THE PAST

I

"The child and the library." The very words have a charm that recalls the opening dreams of life. Or, perhaps, "the child and the book" are words that carry more memories. Possibly of a far-away, vanished pinewood, where, lying under the trees in the hearing of the sea, one made wonderful voyages, excursions and alarums on the perfectly enchanting island with the Swiss family. This, a memory of my own seventh year, is the most vivid literary recollection I possess, and still for me the best place in which to read is a wood. To most it recalls small figures curled up on the rug in front of the winter fireside, who uncurled most unwillingly, aroused from their partnership in fairyland or in thrilling heroisms on sea and on land, for the prosaic business of bath and bed. Indeed, when we glance backward to our earliest years, we shall find that for most of us the things that have endured are not persons or special physical events, but a sunlit meadow somewhere, a strip of beach sizzling in a high wind, a curve of a river that flowed past us once in reality and then for always flowed in our dreams; and, as strong as these impressions, and often scarcely to be disentangled from them, are landscapes, rivers and seas of romance which our books gave to us. If this be a right interpretation of the experience of many of us, is it extravagant to say that apart from the mental and physical attributes which are his by heredity, the most subtly important thing in the life of the child is the book he *reads*? I mean, of course, the book which he reads because he loves it, not the book which parents and others, sometimes quite foolishly, impose upon the child "because it is good for him." Such impositions are never, in any circumstances that I can imagine, *good* for the child. Indeed, the average child is a far wiser chooser of its own books than is the average adult, and we disliked books that we were forced to read just as much as we disliked the medicines that we were forced to swallow. But if the child is given reasonable freedom of choice, which means utter freedom where the field of choice is good, then the book becomes a tremendous factor in his development.

2

The child of to-day is in this matter almost happier than he knows. Authors, publishers and other distributors of books, especially public librarians, bring to him worlds of romance that his fathers were unable to enter. Some even think that too much is given to the child, too many books, with a resultant dissipation of his interests and a destroying of his powers of concentration. Is this true, or is it a product of that adult jealousy which finds its crudest interpretation in such nonsense as: "I had to rough it when I was young, and it won't hurt him to do the same"? One of the disconcerting things is the richness of modern life, and the multiplicity of its interests. The town child is drawn hither and thither a thousand ways; the shops are exhibitions, and there are cinemas, clubs, scout and guide troops, church societies, and school demands. What is left? Even the countryside is invaded by many interests that were unknown only twenty years ago; in fact, in some counties petrol and the internal-combustion engine have left no "country" in the sense in which men of less than middle age knew it in childhood. It follows that leisure, and especially leisure in which concentration is possible, is rarer than it was. The world of books reflects this outside world very clearly. Where the child of old had few books, which were loved and learned by heart; where a Macaulay could say that were all the copies of *Paradise Lost* and *Pilgrim's Progress* lost he could reproduce them from memory, so much had he read them in youth, to-day one child in a thousand has read through *Paradise Lost*, and one in a million could remember half a dozen pages verbatim of either. Some older people affect quite honestly to lament this state of affairs: and one can give a passing sympathy to them. But actualities are our business, not regrets. It may even be permitted to us to doubt if it would be useful to confine any child to *Paradise Lost* and *Pilgrim's Progress* in the hope of making a new Macaulay; it certainly would not be possible. Undoubtedly, however, one of the problems of to-day is how to provide the child, and especially the town child, with leisure to live his own individual, imaginative and spiritual life; and it may be that a large, beautiful room in every district, furnished with books and the means to read them—in short, a properly equipped library—may be a factor in its solution.

3

Whatever the answer to the general question may be, the present happiness of our children in their wealth of literary possessions is of quite recent growth, and has been reached by slow and not altogether painless processes. The children's books, with about a half-dozen exceptions, which are worth a moment's thought are less than a century old. What did all the children read before that time? School books and other works written for their instruction and edification have always existed since the days of Cynewulf and Alfred, as Mr. Harvey Darton reminds us, but he also tells us that children's books in our modern definition—books that children read in their leisure for pleasure and profit—did not exist until very late. "Apart from education, children had no books of their own before the seventeenth century, and very few then." We notice in passing (leaning the while on Mr. Darton) that Ælfric's *Colloquy* is given the life of dialogue which was revived centuries later by Erasmus. The horn-book came into existence in the sixteenth century; a piece of wood shaped like the head of a spade, on which the paper bearing the text was fastened, and over it a guard of transparent horn. Such a small surface would carry only "an alphabet, a short syllabary, and, usually, the Lord's Prayer." The horn-book lasted until late in the eighteenth century, so tenacious of life are articles produced for children; and it was followed by the battledore, which was a folded card with a wood-cut and the elementary sort of text already made familiar on the horn-book.

4

Adults have always been deeply concerned to improve the minds of the young—at any rate so far as literary provision for them has been concerned; but there is an air of professionalism about early books for them, and the mantle of the schoolmaster, the parson and the dire prophet was so rarely laid aside, that we pause to ask where nursery rhymes, folk-tales and other quite ancient possessions of children, came from. The answer is obvious enough, I think. Nine-tenths of the children of the world until not much more than a hundred years ago could not read at all, but parents and elders told tales by the fireside without a doubt from the day pictured by Kipling when the woman set up house in the cave. Ages before the folk-tales were written down children knew fairies, gnomes, witches and dragons, and followed the heroes of all time on their adventures. "Many of these stories," wrote Thackeray, "have been related in their present shape thousands of years ago to little copper-coloured Sanskrit children. The very same tale has been heard by the Northern Vikings as they lay on their shields on deck, and by the Arab crouching under the stars on the Syrian plains, when the flocks were gathered in, and the mares were picketed by their tents."[1] In fact, story-telling is a much earlier and more natural process than story-writing, and some of the best survivals in rhyme and fancy, as, for example, the jingling alphabet, "A was an archer," existed on the tongues of parents, nurses and children at least a century before they were fixed in writing. Even to-day every normal child—and all adults, too—would rather listen to a story than read it; and (in a book on children's libraries) one may point out thus early that one of the best ways to persuade little children to read stories for themselves is to tell the story to them first. They will read in their endeavour to repeat the pleasure they experienced in hearing it. That is the main reason for what is called the "Story Hour" in public and other libraries which we shall have to deal with later.

5

But to return to the somewhat arid and often fearsome literary pathway which children had to tread

[1] *Frazer's Magazine*, 1846.

CHILDREN'S BOOKS OF THE PAST

from the fifteenth almost to the beginning of the nineteenth century: there was a type of book of distinctly secular character, the book of courtesy, the best known of which was *The Babees Book*,[1] dating from the reign of Henry VIII, and consisting mainly of two rhyming treatises, both bearing the name *Boke of Nurture*, by Hugh Rhodes and John Russell respectively. It was the counterpart in its day of Lord Chesterfield's letters, the monitor of the child and adolescent in all usages of polite society, at nobles' houses, at home and at private tutors', at English and foreign universities, and so on. A taste of its quality may be got from a single stanza:—

> A, Bele[2] Babees, herkne now to my lore!
> Whenne yee entre into your lorde's place,
> Say first, "god spede"; And alle that ben byfore
> You in this stede, salue withe humble Face;
> Stert not Rudely; komme Inne an esy pace;
> Holde up youre heede, and knele but on oone kne
> To youre sovereyne or lorde, whe'air he be.

Brighter hours were provided by a type of literature which was parallel in time with the horn-book and battledore. The chap-book was so called because it was peddled from village to village by chapmen, the type of itinerant merchant recalled and ennobled in Wordsworth's *Excursion*, but described by an early lexicographer as "a paltry pedlar who in a long pack or maund which he carries for the

---

[1] Early English Text Society (Edited by Frederick J. Furnivall), 1868.
[2] Fair.

most part hanging from his neck before him, hath almanacks, books of news, and other trifling wares to sell." But the chapman brought the popular tales of Europe in his pack, *Bevis of Southampton, Adam Bell* and *Flores of Greece* amongst those forgotten except by scholars to-day; but also *Beauty and the Beast, Cinderella, Jack and the Beanstalk, Little Red Riding Hood, The Sleeping Beauty, Tom Thumb* and *Dick Whittington*. He sold them for a penny or a halfpenny; sometimes for a farthing. Their production was cruder than that of any "penny dreadful" of the nineteenth century. Their authors are not known; in fact it is probable that they were written down by enterprising scribes from the lips of tale-tellers. They consisted of sixteen or more pages with woodcuts which might illustrate their story, but very often did not, all impressed as badly as might be. As is usual with popular literature, they were not designed in the first place for children; in fact, children were forbidden to read them; which appears in all ages to be a sure way to bringing about their adoption by children. For two and a half centuries, when the official literature for children reeked of gruesome piety and the horrors of the charnel house, the chap-book brought the things that really matter to adults and to children, action and imagination. The chap-book declined in the middle of the eighteenth century, but did not actually disappear until well on into the eighteen-twenties.

CHILDREN'S BOOKS OF THE PAST

6

Contemporaneously with the best period of the proscribed chap-book, and perhaps one cause of its success, was the worst period of the "legitimate" book for the child. Bunyan did to some extent redeem the age with his crude *Divine Emblems: or, Temporal Things Spiritualized*, which was identified in 1889 as an abridged version of his *A Book for Boys and Girls: or, Country Rhimes for Children*, a series of fables about animals and birds with a strong moral attached. In this desire to moralize the child he is at one with the whole of the sixteenth, seventeenth and eighteenth and even the first half of the nineteenth century. His *Pilgrim's Progress*, now a book of books for children, which they discovered for themselves much later as they discovered *Gulliver* and *Robinson Crusoe*, was, like the two latter, never intended for children; and the "inspired tinker" would no doubt have marvelled to hear that two and a half centuries later it would be regarded by many children as their peculiar possession. In *Divine Emblems*, however, he was attempting to give children something original and really designed for them.

Other writers, translating into the mental sphere the belief that "to spare the rod is to spoil the child," wrote books of which the main features are a horribly un-Christ-like piety, infantile virtue rewarded ironically with premature death, and the promise of a hot hell that gaped ever before the feet of little sinners. This view pervades and energizes child literature until the eighteen-thirties, and it was not wholly extinguished within living memory. Did ever the grisly mind of the well-meaning adult express itself more completely than James Janeway did in 1720 or thereabouts in the very title of his *Token for Children: being an Exact Account of the Conversion, Holy and Exemplary Lives, and Joyful Deaths of Several Young Children?* This work is described by Mr. Darton as having been perhaps the most popular of its day. It may be supposed that if a book is bought it is read, but it does not always follow. Were the children of the eighteenth century compelled to read these books? They probably were. It used to be the practice in quite recent times for foolish parents to force small children to read certain books, especially on Sundays, with the result that to many men and women still living some of the finest books in the language are merely repulsive. For most folk a book is good or bad in accord with the circumstances and the atmosphere in which they were first introduced to it. But, even if in many cases children were forced to read the gruesome imaginings of Master James Janeway, there seems to be evidence that children do not invariably dislike death and tears. Sentimental Tommy's absorption in the funeral is very true to child nature. All primitive folk, and most children are primitive, have a macabre strain. There is, therefore, not much to wonder at in the survival of this type for more than a century after Janeway. Thus, in a little volume

CHILDREN'S BOOKS OF THE PAST

published by the Religious Tract Society in 1840 or thereabouts are two lyrics considered eminently suitable for the young mind which I cannot forbear to quote:—

THE BUD

Pretty Bud, I love to see
Much in you resembling me,
And, from your instructive look,
Learn, as from a little book.

I am young, and so are you,
Life with us is fresh and new;
Yet fair buds oft withered lie
And the youngest children die.

etc.

and this equally encouraging gem:—

THE LEAVES

The leaves as they fall
Give a lesson to all,
The low and the high,
That we too must die.

both of which suggest that infant mortality was so universal and so natural a phenomenon that an exclusive attention to the small souls in such rapidly perishing tenements of flesh was the proper business of all grown-ups in their relations with children.

7

It is a relief to meet with John Newberry, who in 1740 recognized the need for real children's books and began to supply it. From St. Paul's Churchyard he issued *The Lilliputian Magazine*, 1751–52, and other works, amongst which were two which are ascribed to the gentle Oliver Goldsmith, *Goody Two-Shoes* with confidence, and *Mother Goose's Melody* and *Mother Goose's Tales* with less certainty. In Newberry we have the beginning of modern publishing for children; he has had many successors. Some of the books they published have little life to-day as compared with those we have just mentioned; but in their day the works of "good Mrs. Trimmer," to use Calverly's name for her,—*Fabulous Histories*, for example,—and Mrs. Sherwood's *Little Henry and His Bearer*, 1815, *The Fairchild Family*, 1818, and *Henry Milner*, 1822, had enormous vogue. Almost contemporaneously the greatest of these writers, Maria Edgeworth, was in her full activity. Her *Parent's Assistant*, 1796, *Moral Tales*, *Harry and Lucy*, and *Frank* have a style and beauty and a sense of construction that the others possess in a much lesser degree. Thomas Day's *Sandford and Merton* lives to-day as the heavy-weight of this school of moral story-tellers. Their morality was immense. They were horrified when contemporaneously the terrible influence of France in the fairy stories of Perrault, Madame D'Aulnoy, and the romance by Berquin (his *L'Ami des Enfants* had been successfully translated) invaded English homes, and their consternation is as laughable to-day as were the recent efforts of some American educationists to suppress the fairy story. There were many writers of this "moral school."

CHILDREN'S BOOKS OF THE PAST

8

The romance for children rose with the romance for the adult. Children gradually appropriated *Pilgrim's Progress, Gulliver's Travels, Robinson Crusoe* and (in 1785) *Munchausen's Travels*. When in 1819 Scott produced *Ivanhoe*, they appropriated that also, and it was only a natural step towards books of the same type but in more elementary form. We can trace on one hand the novel in its various forms for the adult and on the other see growing side by side with it something resembling those forms for younger readers. A contemporaneous and most influential factor in this development was the modern chap-book, as we may call it, the "penny dreadful," or "blood" or "horrible," as it was variously named. This was an ill-printed publication with garish wrappers, introducing the delectable adventures of certain stock characters, such as Jack Harkaway, Jack Sheppard and Dick Turpin the highwaymen; Buffalo Bill, the scout, hunter and fighter of redskins; and Frank Reed, the inventor. Sexton Blake, the imitation Sherlock Holmes, is more recent and survives enough exploits to fill the lifetimes of a score of Methuselahs. Some of these were of astonishing virility; some raised vice and law-breaking to such admirable heights that magistrates attributed much boy-crime to their influence, and parents forbade them as they forbade chap-books of old. They exercised a great influence on the modern book for boys which began with such writers as

Ballantyne and James Greenwood, and, through Fenn and Henty, has brought us to Westerman, Strang and Brereton to-day. An understanding of the psychology of these cheap ever-popular works is of first importance, and we shall pursue the matter further in the next chapter.

9

In 1824 Grimm's fairy stories reached England, and a little later Mary Howitt made Hans Andersen a household word. The bad days, at least for the well-to-do child, were rapidly passing. The writers who contributed to the new literature for children were not very many, but we have no space to deal comprehensively with them here. It must, however, be mentioned that Grimm and Andersen were the natural inspirers of Ruskin's *King of the Golden River*, Kingsley's *Water Babies*, George MacDonald's *At the Back of the North Wind*, and Thackeray's *The Rose and the Ring*, although these are all original tales and not folk-lore stories as were those of the brothers Grimm. Then came Lewis Carroll, to bring writing for children to almost perfection in *Alice in Wonderland*, 1866, and *Alice's Adventures Underground*, 1872, which with (at a distance) *Sylvie and Bruno*, 1889, have never been surpassed as works for certain types of children. That tradition lives to-day. In *Peter and Wendy*, 1911, Barrie has caught the light and reflected it in his own inimitable way; and only yesterday, in the adventures of toys and

CHILDREN'S BOOKS OF THE PAST

pets such as gave Alice her romance, but those of our own children, Alan Alexander Milne has given another almost perfect classic to the nursery in *Winnie-the-Pooh*, 1926. But they are the vanguards of a very great company.

AUTHORITIES

BARRY, FLORENCE V. A Century of Children's Books. 1922. Methuen.

DARTON, F. J. HARVEY. Children's Books. *In* The Cambridge History of English Literature, Vol. XI, pp. 366–87. 1914. (Bibliography, pp. 475–92).

FIELD, E. M. The Child and His Book: some account of the History and Progress of Children's Literature in England. Illus. 1891. Wells, Gardner.

TUER, ANDREW W. Pages and Pictures from Forgotten Children's Books. Illus. 1898–9. Leadenhall Press.

—— Stories from Old Fashioned Children's Books. Illus. 1899–1900. Leadenhall Press.

WELCH, CHARLES. Children's Books That Have Lived. *In* The Library. Ser. 2, Vol. I, pp. 314–23. 1900.

CHAPTER II

WHAT CHILDREN READ TO-DAY

I

Although we have by no means exhausted the history of children's books, they have become as it were a stream of such volume and with so many ramifying channels that a guide to them becomes necessary. Criticism, as Mr. Harvey Darton remarks, must replace history. We must therefore attempt something in the way of an account of the qualities of children's books as we now see them. Of criticism of such books in any exact sense there has been until quite recently little or none. The more general literary reviews have not shown themselves able to deal with them in any intelligent way; and critics appear to have found the work of discriminating them either impossible or unprofitable. If you have any doubt on this subject, turn to the column labelled compendiously "Books for the Young" or "Gift Books" in the most reputable review known to you, and set yourself to learn from it such simple matters as: the style in which the book is written; the age of the child to whom it will appeal and what sort of preliminary knowledge is necessary to its right understanding; its truth or otherwise to the life it purports to describe;

the quality of its characterization, its humour, and morality in the widest sense of this much abused term; its physical production: printing type; the quality of its illustrations; the quality of the paper on which it is printed; and the strength of its sewing and binding. The results will be illuminating in their almost completely negative character. It may be argued that all that concerns the critic is the book as a work of art; and children's books are rarely such, and may be neglected. This is nonsense and like most nonsense is quite untrue. *Alice in Wonderland*, a great children's book, is as to literary style, imagination and construction a fine work of art, and in its earlier editions—those in crown-octavo, with Tenniel's illustrations, printed on a tough imitation art paper which took those illustrations perfectly, with its sound gold edges, strong linen thread sewing, and red stout cloth bevel-edged case—was physically as fine a book as has ever appeared for children. It is surely as worth while to bring out these invaluable facts about a book as to say that it is "exciting," "thrilling," or that "no normal boy or girl will be able to resist it," and other similar foolishness which sometimes pretends to be an account of children's books.

The matter is surely urgent, even vital, if any of the implications with which we started this book are true. It is also surely possible to lay down some principles of criticism such as are indicated by the questions we were to ask of our review. Such criticism, I think, will deal with the inner or literary, or, if I may use the term, the spiritual quality of a book, the work as art; and with its physical or bodily quality, the work as craftsmanship.

In dealing with both art and craftsmanship we have to bear in mind that the age of the children is an important factor. With books for the adult the question of the age of the reader is probably of no great consequence, but even this is doubtful, as age may indicate a stage of culture or literary or other receptivity. For example, a man who has never read poetry until his fortieth year is not likely to make much of it afterwards, but will be blind in an important mental direction, as indeed many men are! It is probable, however, that the mental divergences of adults are not so many as are those of the child from the time at which he becomes conscious of books to the age of sixteen or thereabouts. This requires us to define what we really mean by children in our discussion. Childhood ranges from infancy to early adolescence;[1] and as this is a book for practical librarians, we may fix "children's libraries" as being libraries for young people from the age at which they can enjoy pictures—four or thereabouts, perhaps a little earlier—to the age when, it is to be hoped, adult books will appeal to them—sixteen, or, again, it may be a little earlier. I am altogether opposed to age limits in libraries unless they are essential for disciplinary or other administrative reasons which cannot other-

---

[1] J. W. Slaughter in his *The Adolescent* defines it as from the age of puberty to twenty-eight. This is hardly the range of a children's library.

WHAT CHILDREN READ TO-DAY

wise be met. There are no such mental divisions of children as lists of books suitable for this or that age would seem to imply. I say *seem*, advisedly, as no compiler of such lists known to me has ever demanded that children of such and such an age should be limited to such and such books. This is true of course only as between groups of years as from 6 to 8, from 9 to 11, and from 12 to 15, because while the boy of 6 may be and usually is widely different from him of 8, it is clear that 6 can rarely be like 12, although in a few special cases, of rapid development on one side and of arrested development on the other, the ages tend to be alike. We have to assume that there are little children, children, and older children, a classification the inadequacy of which I regret but which there seems to be no escaping. Then there is a slightly different rate of development in literary appreciation, or at any rate demand, in the two sexes, which must be borne in mind in any adequate study of the subject.

In order to clarify the subject, I will try to deal with a few general principles first, and will return to more special points. A tabular list of qualities is ugly, but may be useful.

THE BOOK AS ART

1. A book must have literary style, or at least good English.
2. It must have wholesome imagination.
3. It must be true.
4. It must be law-abiding.
5. It must have a right sense of wit and humour.

A MANUAL OF CHILDREN'S LIBRARIES
THE BOOK AS CRAFTSMANSHIP

1. It must be on a slightly yellow paper with correct margins.
2. The type must be large enough.
3. The illustrations must be good and in correct register.
4. It must be sewn with linen thread through its folds, not with steel wire, and must never be stabbed.
5. It must be cased in good cloth over sound boards.

Literary quality is obtainable in children's books, but is often wanting. The average beginner in authorship usually attempts the writing of a child's book, as is quite natural as nearly all authors who are destined to succeed commence their literary apprenticeship at an age when they are nearest in their tastes to the books of their teens. Many such books, although a small percentage of those written, are published, and crudity of style is often the result. It is almost impossible to select a whole library of books which do possess style; it is even doubtful if we know so perfectly what we mean by the quality that we always recognize it when we see it. My own experience suggests that it should be sought for, of course, because we want children to know the joy that lives in the deft and beautiful use of words; but all we can really be sure about is that our books are at least grammatical. A surer criticism of children's books will give us style in time; we hope so at least.

The other conditions laid down that a book must have a wholesome quality of imagination, be law-abiding and be truthful, are perhaps almost equally difficult of adequate definition. Wholesome imagination and truth are collateral qualities, and here at once we encounter two definite types of child literature which exercise the minds of adults in strange ways, the fairy story and the primitive type of literature which we used to call the *"Penny dreadful,"* although specimens of it can no longer be bought for a penny and it is often less "dreadful" than many books which apparently have the approval of grown-ups.

To take the fairy tale first: is it wholesome, and is it true? In some American schools, staffed apparently wholly by women, the momentous conclusion has been reached that it is neither. Fairies do not exist; they mislead the child's imagination, therefore; in some way they are inimical; they must be banished from nursery and school. The conclusion would be ludicrous if it were not likely to be translated into action by enthusiastic reformers whose perceptions of imagination and truth are muddled. The very notion is clearly an adult impertinence. It is impossible to imagine any child in England being robbed of its heritage in, say, Cinderella, because some foolish adult has made the discovery that fairy queens do not exist and that pumpkins cannot as a rule be metamorphosized into fine coaches. It may be too that there *are* fairy tales with a grain of the coarse in them; but I have yet to learn of any child who has been led into evil courses by them or who even recognized that evil existed in them. They are true to the imaginative life of childhood, the time of dreams, and such a

No. 1 Joy Street, Liverpool
Lent by the Liverpool Public Libraries

story as Cinderella is highly moral. The matter need not be pursued.

The penny "dreadful," "horrible" or "blood" is in a different category. My acquaintance with it is fairly extensive, seeing that I have read with interest, and at one time with undisguised relish, with the acquiescence if not with the approval of a good schoolmaster, samples of Deadwood Dick, Buffalo Bill, Frank Reed, Nick Carter, Sexton Blake and many others whose once famous names I no longer recollect. There is an excellent case to be made for them. I once heard Dr. T. J. Macnamara say that "every boy worth his salt read every one he could lay his hands upon." This, in spite of the fact that these novelettes have been the literary "whipping-boys" of many magistrates and other mentors of youth who have traced youthful misdoings to much reading of them. As every boy read them, it was natural that they played some part in their mental make-up. I do not wish to underrate this view—which has now been transferred to the cinema—because there are grades of penny dreadfuls as there are of all other kinds of literature. Certainly there appears to be a type of which I have no personal knowledge, never having encountered a specimen, although I was told quite recently that they are sold late on Saturday nights on the market stalls of my own town; but I could never find them by day! These apparently deal with the beauty of defiance of law, with illicit sex matters and so on. They seem to exist in America judging

WHAT CHILDREN READ TO-DAY

by the experience of Mr. W. T. Field, whose excellent *A Guide to Literature* may be commended to all who are interested in our subject. He describes them as "news-stand tales, reeking with sensational boy bandit stories, tales of the slums and of the brothel, as well as of alluring vice in high life." Mr. Field also tells a gruesome story of their effects. He asked a truant officer in an American city what he thought were the effects of this literature and was shown a well-thumbed assortment of it, with such titles as *Three Bad Men*, *Tracy the Bandit*, and the *Life of Jessie James*, which the officer had confiscated. He was also shown a drawer full of weapons obtained similarly.

"Lifting out a revolver, he handed it to me. 'Perhaps this is the best answer I can give you,' he said. The revolver had a card attached to it, on which was written, 'Death to Solie Cohen, 401, West Taylor Street, shot by Abe Abrams, thirteen years of age, while playing Jessie James in Mrs. Cohen's kitchen.' Another class of reading matter, even more dangerous to our youth than 'hold-up' stories, consists of tales of Paris and New York by night, dealing in the most insinuating way with a kind of life which has already gained too much publicity in the daily press."

I am ignorant of such "bloods," and must accept Mr. Field's view of them. Those I do know are familiar to everyone; they are written by journeyman writers. I am told even by schoolmasters and clergy, who are paid from £5 to £25, as will be seen by *The Writers' Year-Book*, for a story of forty thousand words introducing a series of stock characters. For example, Sexton Blake, and his wonderful boy assistant, Tinker, have four forty-thousand word adventures monthly, and must in the time measurement of their adventures have lived through several centuries, as I have suggested. These tales are sometimes quite well written. I met with a description of a foggy night in London in a Sexton Blake story which in its vividness recalled the fog in *Bleak House*, and was, moreover, in really good English. In addition, "something happens" on every page, almost in every paragraph, and, on the moral side, vice always fails most ignominiously, and virtue, truth, and courage triumph gloriously in these stories. Their morality is good. They err on the side of probability, or, rather, the want of it. On the physical side they are usually produced in small double-columned type on the poorest paper and have the crudest illustrations. We hear of boys outwitting bad but brilliant statesmen and the cleverest of rogues with a courage and facility which are laughable when related to reality. One boy of fourteen merely circumvents Napoleon quite easily! One may sum up the case against them. Their style, if good sometimes, is more often bad. They are inimical to the sense of proportion in their readers, seeing that their improbabilities, manifest to some adults, are not always so to youngsters. They destroy the sense of beauty which should come from books, and they are obviously destructive of eyesight.

WHAT CHILDREN READ TO-DAY

The case for them is equally instructive. Action and incident are the demands of the child both in his physical and mental life. He gets them here. The long descriptions dear to the classical novelist are merely irritating delays in the movement of the only thing that matters, the story. And modern life is more rapid than it was, and the child wants literature which paces with it. He loved Henty once, but Henty has no airplanes, sixty miles an hour is for him a terrible speed, his wars are small in the shadow of the Great War; Henty is read, but no longer with the avidity with which as a boy I read him. That is typical; the child wants excitement: "It's a daft book," says Wee Macgregor, "naebody gets kilt in it!" All this is no doubt unfortunate, and we librarians must do what we can to urge upon children as unobtrusively as may be that there is a life of the past and present in books which is not one rush from incident to incident. But it is a slow and gradual process, and the case of the reader for his most popular literature must be understood before we can attempt it.

To begin at an earlier stage. We may surround little children with beautiful books which we think ought to rejoice them; but we shall often find, if we do not definitely prevent it, that their next coppers will be expended upon one of three papers which may usefully be named, *The Rainbow, Tiger Tim's Weekly* and *The Playbox*, all of which come from one publishing house to whom they must bring literally golden returns. These are not bad papers, although they are below the level of the children's library as I see it. My reader probably knows them; they illustrate, in a series of pictures in pink and black, with the briefest simple text, various adventures, the principal ones being those of a school kept by a bear, Mrs. Bruin—a grown-up Teddy Bear obviously—whose pupils are nursery animals, Tiger Tim, Jumbo the elephant, Jacko the monkey, Joey the parrot and so on. The adventures are usually some form of mischievous trick, such as getting out of bed on Christmas Eve to raid the pantry, or putting snow in the bath. At the height of their "innocent pleasures," Mrs. Bruin enters, arrests the merriment, and imposes punishment, usually in the shape of extra lessons.

In analysis it seems to me that the inventor of these periodicals had a fairly sound perception of at least the outlines of the psychology of the child. Toys are living things to children; they do have such adventures together, and they are usually interrupted by the adult in the manner suggested. *Tiger Tim* is in the pedigree of some of the finest of children's books, and may possibly be used as a stepping-stone to them; it is at least worth trial. The child without access to works of a *like* character will continue to read these periodicals for a very long time; but I believe that if he will read them he will also read the adventures of the toy animals in such books as Beatrix Potter's *Story of Peter Rabbit*; may be led then to Milne's most attractive adventures of similar nursery friends in *Winnie-the-*

WHAT CHILDREN READ TO-DAY

Pooh and its companion volumes; and what are these but leads to Carroll's *Alice* and the *Jungle Books* of Kipling? There seems here to be a sequence of some value to the directors of children's reading. To prevent a child from reading a lower form of literature without providing a higher, equally attractive, equivalent, is the poorest policy and means defeat; but the sequence suggested may mean success.

To continue the experiment. If Sexton Blake is an imitation Sherlock Holmes, will not his reader like the real thing as well as the imitation? Doyle did not write for children, but he wrote well and boys appreciate him. In like manner, the boy who wants the adventure type of "blood" can be given *Treasure Island*, where he will get all the adventure and bloodshed he wants but will get it in the purest of style; the blood will be good blood. But even *Treasure Island* deals with two centuries since, and for the boy who is unfortunately so "modern" in his outlook that he cannot appreciate it, there is the prince of modern penny dreadfuls in John Buchan's *Thirty-Nine Steps*, to give him every thrill in a world which he can see around him.

I do not pretend to have envisaged the whole process, but it appears to me that a library which is going to attract children and to lead them to the appreciation of the best in literature must be based on a recognition of the known tastes of children; that authors who aspire to write for them must begin with a close study of the lower forms of literature to which they naturally turn, and must then produce similar things with greater truth, better style, and more artistry. This is a far better course than to attempt to force great books upon immature minds. If a child does not like Scott or Dickens, or any great writers, it is usually because he is not ready for them. I do not suggest that penny dreadfuls should be stocked in libraries, or that their reading should in any circumstances be encouraged. I do think, however, that a children's librarian should herself have sufficient personal acquaintance with them, to enable her to direct the taste for them in her readers to what she believes to be wiser ends.

I think what we mean by truth in children's books can be inferred from what has been discussed. Adventures are frequently improbable, but they ought not to be entirely impossible; they should be within the range of somebody's possible experience. There are those who object to stories of animals who talk and possess human characteristics; but if this is not true of the natural animal, it is true of the animal in the child's experience; his pets all have distinct personalities. The adult is too prone to project his own knowledge, and sometimes materialism, into the world of the child. The normal child is perfectly well aware of the difference between fact and the romance life he lives with animals and toys!

That a book must be law-abiding will be generally agreed. It must not bring into ridicule the

WHAT CHILDREN READ TO-DAY

wholesome human relationships; must recognize the rights of men and of animals; it should show cruelty its own hideous features; it ought not to make the discomfiture of the good, the old, the poor or the deformed a matter of rejoicing; it ought to strengthen the bond between parent and child, and so on. Books with brutal fathers, unkind mothers, sneaking schoolmasters and such like enormities cannot be law-abiding in any sense that we care to recognize. Most decent authors, however, conform to the standard in these matters.

The wit and humour of children's books are a subtle matter. Little children find astonishing humour in phrases and curious words. One of the funniest verses ever heard by two little children I know of seven and four is in *At the Zoo* by Milne:—

There are badgers and bidgers and bodgers, and a Superintendents' House,
There are masses of goats, and a Polar, and different kinds of mouse,
And I think there's a sort of something which is called a wallaboo—
But I gave buns to the elephant when I went down to the Zoo.

The syllables of "wallaboo" always produced shouts of laughter. Milne's use of an occasional long word, too, as in "the bees are 'suspicious,'" makes much appeal, as certainly do the names of his other mysterious animals, the "Wizzle," and "Woozle," and his remarkably elusive "heffalump." At a somewhat later stage, humour of a grotesque type appeals, long noses, deformities and similar matters being special favourites, and the essence of humour an old lady falling off a chair. I have seen a whole audience of children go into something like convulsions when a picture of Walter Raleigh, wearing an Elizabethan ruff, has been shown on the lantern screen. The deductions to be made, if any can be made from such experiences, are that the child, from the nines to twelves, at any rate, likes crude humour. Much of it would be intolerable if found in actual life, and it is worth while to endeavour to provide books from which the objectionable sorts are absent.

A later chapter will deal with book selection in its practical aspects, but here it may be urged that the basis of a children's library are the great prose works of imagination which were written for them or which generations of children have appropriated. It may be that there are a score of such books, and certainly there will be no general agreement as to the whole of them, although for most of them there will be. They should be within the reach of all boys and girls before they come to the age of twelve. They may not all be read; but the opportunity should be there. Tentatively, I would suggest these books as essential. The reader may add others:—

> Æsop's Fables.
> Alcott. Little Women.
> Andersen's Fairy Tales.
> Arabian Nights' Entertainments.
> Barrie. Peter and Wendy.

WHAT CHILDREN READ TO-DAY

    Bunyan. Pilgrim's Progress.
    Carroll. Alice in Wonderland.
    Defoe. Robinson Crusoe.
    Grimm's Fairy Tales.
    Hawthorne. Tanglewood Tales.
    Kingsley. Water Babies.
    Kipling. Just So Stories and Jungle Books.
    Milne. Winnie-the-Pooh.
    Ruskin. King of the Golden River.
    Stevenson. Treasure Island.
    Swift. Gulliver's Travels.

I am prepared to agree with anyone who says that I ought to have included *Tom Sawyer*, *Uncle Remus*, *The Wind in the Willows*, and many others, but I am perfectly certain that none of those I have included ought to be omitted. They are the foundation literature of childhood.

A word may be written about the difference we find in the reading of girls as compared with boys. Books for girls have not been written in any numbers until quite recently, and they do not compare very favourably with those for boys. As a result until she is about twelve the girl prefers the book written for her brother. Librarians discover that the girl develops her reading tastes rather earlier than the boy; the miss who found fairies fascinating at seven, revels in the school or adventure story at twelve, and is deep in the love romance soon after fourteen; while the boy has generally the profoundest distaste for the last-named type of literature until at least two or three years later. Some older girls show a curious desire for sad books, one I know expressed a desire for "hospital stories with operations," and there is a distinct enjoyment of sentimental sorrows. It is certainly questionable whether such a taste is to be encouraged. Lately, Angela Brazil, with her somewhat unvarying school tales, has drawn the young girl. One experienced children's librarian has expressed interesting views about this: "With girls Angela Brazil is still the favourite—why it is hard to say. Andrew Lang—the fairy books—came second and Lewis Carroll third. *Alice* is to the girls what *Peter Pan* is to the boys. Alcott is still much in demand—especially *Little Women*. The thing that impressed me when going through the voting papers[1] was the fact that boys have a much more catholic taste than girls. The average girl begins by reading fairy stories, goes straight from these to school stories, and unfortunately seems to stop there—at any rate while she is in the junior library. As a rule she is finished with fairy stories at about ten years. If from then till the time she is fifteen she reads school stories (five years at an average of one book per week) is it to be wondered at that she can digest nothing very nourishing when she ascends to the senior library?" There appears to be room for much thought and experiment in this question of girls' books.

A question of a rather serious nature is the age at which children should be permitted to read the

[1] This extract is from an article by Miss Gladys Willton, "What Children Read," in *The Library World*, Vol. XXXII, p. 227. She discusses the results of a census in her library in which 1,021 children answered the question, What is your favourite book?

more virile books written for adults. Many of these deal with matters which can scarcely be regarded as suitable for children; but there is little need for apprehension in the matter. If a child has access to a large library he will readily discover the books most desirable for himself, and, as in the majority of cases with the penny dreadful, the evil passes him by. Indeed, Ruskin's opinion that no noble child has ever been injured by a work of fiction may be accepted with little qualification; and we have known children to read books which have dealt with the most difficult problems of life, and to rise from them completely oblivious of the nature of the scenes which are so patent to their older readers. The innocence of the child is his main safeguard against evil here as everywhere, and there is much to be said for the point of view that the child who receives harm from a book of this character had already become unwholesomely wise from other sources; the evil is already done. Recognizing all this, however, it is undoubtedly true that any vicious tendency in childhood may be kept alive by unsuitable books, and it is wise to exclude any book about which reasonable doubt is felt. The conclusion of the whole matter is that few books of unsuitable character make any real appeal to young readers.

Our library must of course go beyond fiction; must contain books on all subjects, so far as they exist, within the classification given in Chapter IX. Here we are on ground which is at once firmer and more difficult. On the positive side we can be sure that the book of sociology, religion, science or travel that is written for the child must possess the same qualities of modernity, accuracy, style and good production that we require in such books for adults. Ruskin said that bad books of this kind were more harmful by far than bad fiction. It was probably from a similar reasoning that Bernard Shaw declared somewhat cryptically that the best library for children was one that had no children's books in it. "Books that children will read," although not primarily for them, are some of the best for our purpose. Works of travel, history, science in its more popular forms, on the arts and the trades, of essays, poetry and some drama, all originally written for adults, can be examined for their suitability for the library. Scott's Antarctic voyages, Stanley's *In Darkest Africa*, and White's *Natural History of Selborne* are examples of works that are obviously useful. There are, however, large numbers of well-written, well-illustrated works now published for young readers in all classes; and it is essential that the qualities mentioned should be sought for in choosing them. There is also much rubbish, and "paste and scissors literature," designed by enterprising publishers for children, which must be avoided.

This discussion, though longer than I contemplated making it, is still unsatisfactory, because the data upon which definite judgment can be based is lacking. Criticism, as I have affirmed, is still in an

WHAT CHILDREN READ TO-DAY

elementary state, and there is as yet no sound system of the psychology of child reading. The studies of Terman and Lima in America are confined to books read by children in schools and from school libraries under the eye of the teacher, and are therefore not studies of the child in altogether free and quite natural conditions. We have yet to trace in the history of many child readers the development of individual literary tastes, and this can only be done when a knowledge of the child's heredity, home environment, school experiences and leisure occupations are brought into relation with his choice of books, and their interdependence and reciprocal influences studied. We do not know yet with any certainty—although we may shrewdly suspect—why the child with one type of experience can enjoy *Alice* or the *Jungle Book*, while another child with other experience finds them unreadable. We have never traced the history of the reading of a number of people from six to thirty, and deduced from facts its influence on character and action; although everyone tacitly assumes that the reading of good books somehow leads to good character and success. Until such experiments are made on a continuous scale, and with many individuals, much of the theorizing on reading must remain merely that. But we librarians would like to feel that we were taking part in a scientific use of the reading habit, and I hope that children's librarians will pose their experiences in common with parents and with teachers until we have enough material to form judgments and to draw that guidance which all who influence the reading of the child at present so painfully need. At present we need fewer theories and more facts.

AUTHORITIES

BOARD OF EDUCATION. The Teaching of English. 1921. H.M. Stationery Office.

BOSTWICK, ARTHUR E. How Librarians Choose Books. *In his* Library Essays. 1920. New York: H. W. Wilson.

FIELD, WALTER TAYLOR. A Guide to Literature for Children. 1928. New York: Ginn.

LEGLER, HENRY M. Library Work with Children. *In his* Library Ideals. 1918. Chicago: Open Court.

JAST, LOUIS STANLEY. The Child as Reader. 1927. Libraco.

TERMAN, LOUIS M., and LIMA, MARGARET. Children's Reading: a guide for parents and teachers. 1926. Appleton.

CHAPTER III

THE BOOK AS CRAFTSMANSHIP

I

In turning to discuss the physical qualities of children's books, we must remember that trade conditions often impose limitations on publications which make the ideal book in the material sense rather rare. A really well-produced book, unless it commands an immense sale, cannot be a cheap one, and obviously there is a limit that must not be exceeded in the price of children's books. For some years before the War endeavours were made to improve the quality of book-production generally, which had greatly deteriorated in the first ten years of the century; but the War, with its diversion of all activities to the carrying on of the struggle, almost strangled the paper-trade, and books were issued, by no fault of their publishers, which were on paper made entirely of wood-pulp or even more transient materials, which frayed at a touch, turned yellow in a few weeks and fell to pieces in a few more. Things are better now, but the progress of ten years has not brought us back altogether to the book-production of the eighteen-eighties and nineties. A glance at the first editions of Henty or Fenn as issued by Blackie will illustrate my meaning. Here was a good smooth-surfaced, solid paper with a fair percentage of rag in it, slightly cream in tint, which was sewn with good linen thread, and bore it well; the illustrations were well set in the book; the type was sharp and clear; there were spacious, but not wasteful, margins; the olivine edges kept out the dust; and the covers had thick boards, with bevelled edges and gold-stamped titles. Such a book, of four hundred pages, could be bought for five, or at the most six shillings—a good price in those days. The article, however, was worth twice the cost of any book that purports to rival it to-day.

2

The reasons for present conditions lie in the primary materials of the paper. Linen rag is not used to any extent, if at all, in making ordinary book-papers, although it is employed in making the best writing papers, and on its presence the tensile strength and durability of papers depend. Even before the War featherweight papers were in vogue for many popular books, and they could be made thick and light, and made small books look big and "worth the money." A well-made book is never thick unless it has many pages; that is a lesson that is worth the learning. Some publishers have catered for the taste for large books; they find that buyers in general appear to think that 100 pages on a padded paper are more desirable than 150 on a thinner and may be better paper. The librarian knows that these thick papers are spongy, brittle, friable, and will

THE BOOK AS CRAFTSMANSHIP

not hold the stitches with which they are sewn. The Library Association has a Committee devoted to the "Durability of Paper," which, after examining and experimenting with the various materials, has issued a report[1] which it is hoped will influence both manufacturers and buyers of books to use and demand better paper. Meanwhile, although the individual children's librarian can have only a small influence on the matter, I think he or she should know the qualities recommended. A good book-paper, then, is never quite white, but is of a slightly cream colour; it has a smooth but not a reflecting surface; indeed, it is better that it should be slightly granulated in appearance rather than shiny.

3

The next thing we require in a children's book is that it shall be properly printed. The children's librarian has many responsibilities, but none more certain than the avoiding of books with type which is too small, in which the type lines are too short or too long, or in which the type is worn and gives uneven impressions. I have heard it urged that children read cheap, small-printed serials without any apparent subsequent ill-results. On the other hand, the British Association found it desirable in 1913 to issue *The Report on the Influence of School Books Upon Eyesight*,[2] and the Board of Education's *Report*

[1] *The Durability of Paper: Report of the Special Committee set up by the Library Association*, 1930. London: Library Association.
[2] London Office of the British Association, Burlington House.

A MANUAL OF CHILDREN'S LIBRARIES

of the Consultative Committee on Books in Public Elementary Schools, 1928[1] laid special stress on the need for good book materials of which the type is most important. In a very important, if not entirely conclusive, *Report on the Legibility of Print* by R. L. Pyke, prepared for the Medical Research Council of the Privy Council in 1926,[2] the type most generally agreed to be ideal is described as: "simple, fairly broad, with fairly thick limbs, but not too much contrast in thickness and thinness, and with fairly wide spacing." It will be found that the size of the type, although very important, is not so vital as simplicity and clearness of printing; badly inked type, the often unclean productions of unskilfully worked linotype presses, and works printed from worn stereoplates are all injurious, aesthetically, of course, but undoubtedly also to the eyesight. It is a definite crime—I choose my words—for a librarian to include in a children's library any great or popular book printed in a way that would bring any of these criticisms against it, and it is certainly bad business.

A well-printed book can, in part, be judged by the positions of its margins. Opening such a book we find that the smallest margin is at the top of the page, the largest at the bottom, and the two inner margins together should at least equal each of the side margins. Of course too wide margins may be

---
[1] Stationery Office.
[2] Medical Research Council's Special Report, Series No. 110, Stationery Office.

THE BOOK AS CRAFTSMANSHIP

a sign of padding or of printing artistry; common sense will decide that; but books with inadequate margins should not be bought as these are uneconomical and will prevent the book being re-bound easily.

4

Librarians and educationists generally are by no means agreed upon the value of illustrations in children's books. The Board of Education's *Report on Books in Elementary Schools*, already referred to, expresses the view that many children's books are more elaborately illustrated than is necessary, but the main objection to the elaborateness appears to be that they increase the cost of production.[1] "Illustrations," this Report says, "are essential in books for infants and young children." No one can doubt that, seeing that the young child uses books well before he can read words; is often able to repeat such stories as *Peter Rabbit* from end to end, using the illustrations as clues; as a result, of course, of hearing the book read. The difficulty of illustrations lies in their appearance in works of the imagination. To illustrate *Cinderella*, *The Arabian Nights* or *King Arthur* is to substitute someone else's conception of the characters for the much more valuable and vivid creation of the reader himself. At the same time, it must be admitted that children love pictures even in story books, and theories should, to some extent, give place to this quite obvious love for them.

[1] P. 22.

Books of fact, on geography, history, the sciences and useful arts, must, of course, be illustrated. A well-illustrated book has its illustrations in close relation to the text they illustrate and not scattered anywhere in the book as sometimes happens. The illustrations should be good artistically and true as representations of facts, and in printing they should be clean, with the colours, if any, in perfect "register"; i.e. exactly superposed. An illustration in colours is printed three or four and sometimes more times, one colour over another, and unless the blocks carrying the colours fall into precisely the same position on the paper the print will be out of register and the illustration blurred. Coloured illustrations frequently demand a special "art" paper, and sometimes receive it, but very often one-sided or imitation-art papers are used. In fact the commonest way to illustrate a book in black and white or any colour is to print the illustration on this art paper, which has a preparation of clay on its surface and disintegrates at the least touch of damp, and to tip these illustrations with paste or glue into a book which is printed on another kind of paper altogether. These illustrations come out on the least provocation. The best books for children are printed on a paper sufficiently smooth to take plain half-tone blocks readily. The illustrations then form an integral part of the book. Such books are always to be preferred. The works of Mr. A. A. Milne, with their illustrations by Mr. Ernest H. Shepard, are admirable examples.

THE BOOK AS CRAFTSMANSHIP

5

We can exercise little control at present over the binding, or rather, case-making, of books for children. Sewing and forwarding and case-making are all done by machinery on mass production principles, except in very few instances. A well-made book is, as we have seen in the last chapter, sewn through its folds with stout linen thread, and the sewing is held by strong tapes and mull to the cover. Too often, however, brown paper and glue hold the stitches together and mull of the flimsiest type, reinforced only by the end-papers, forms the connexion between the book and its cover. Better work can only come with an increased appreciation of the art of book-making, and a willingness to pay for it; and improvements in bookbinding machinery are to be expected. It is useless to hope for the old hand-sewing of fifty years ago.

6

In summary, the children's librarian should always prefer the well-made, well-printed and well-illustrated book, however plain it may be in result, to attractive book covers which may hide bad paper, poor printing and inaccurate illustrations. I return to my first argument in this chapter: a good book is rarely cheap. I remember one Education Committee laying down that books should not be bought if they have cost more than a certain modest sum of money.

A MANUAL OF CHILDREN'S LIBRARIES

Any such rule appeals strongly to the local economist, but it is the negation of common sense when applied to books for children. One may buy a copy of Andersen's *Fairy Tales* for 1s., but it has not one per cent. of the value of an edition that can be bought for 7s. 6d., either as a translation or as a work of art or of literature. It appears to me that only the best is really good enough for the children's library.

AUTHORITIES

BOARD OF EDUCATION. Report of the Consultative Committee on Books in Public Elementary Schools. 1928. H.M. Stationery Office.
—— Suggestions for the Consideration of Teachers . . . of Public Elementary Schools. 1923. H.M. Stationery Office.
BROWN, J. D. Manual of Bibliography. 1906. Routledge.
COUTTS, HENRY T., and STEPHEN, G. A. Manual of Library Bookbinding: practical and historical. 1911. Libraco.
HITCHCOCK, F. H. (*Ed.*). The Building of a Book. T. W Laurie.
PYKE, R. L. The Legibility of Print.·Privy Council, Medical Research Council, Special Report Series, No. 110. 1926. H.M. Stationery Office.

CHAPTER IV

BOOK SELECTION AND ACCESSION

I

A practical account of the manner in which books are selected and ordered may come here appropriately. We have seen the qualities we require in books and have formed some conclusions as to our objects in making a library. A library is a balanced collection of productive books. Our books must be good ones and be selected in a catholic manner so that all subjects suitable for youngsters are represented. In this work use should be made of classification, as described in Chapter IX, and of the experience of all who can contribute to the work. Always consult the work of other librarians. The classification of the book suggestions enables us to balance our purchases and in a classified library to judge of the representation of subjects, its sufficiency and modernity. As for the experience of other librarians: there are a number of guides to the choice of children's books, and the best of these are given at the end of this chapter. An examination and comparison of these will give assurance that no really vital book is overlooked in the building up of the library.

2

The proportions of a children's library book stock cannot be set out with anything like finality. I should allow at least 60 per cent. of the books to be stories of one kind or another: possibly more in some districts: and of the whole stock about 60 per cent. should be for children between the ages of nine and thirteen and 20 per cent. for those under and 20 per cent. for those over this range of years. These figures may seem doubtful to those people who have qualms about fiction. There are some who advocate the exclusion of all fiction from children's libraries, and a well-meaning lady actually advocated this course at the Brighton Conference of the Library Association in 1929. This may be mentioned in passing as an extreme view, but some may think that less should be given to fiction.

3

For current books watch should be kept of all periodicals that review children's books. Though they do it badly as a rule they serve as indications. All publishers' catalogues should be requisitioned and examined; and, of course, readers, teachers, parents—and the children themselves—should be invited to suggest books. All suggestions from the children are not necessarily to be accepted, but my experience is that they are usually well worth encouraging, and a notice to the effect that "the

BOOK SELECTION AND ACCESSION

librarian keeps a book in which you may write the titles of books you wish to read" has produced useful results and has interested the children. Our factors, given in the previous paragraph, are based upon the available literature rather than upon any ideal scheme. In all classes other than Literature, and sometimes in that, care should be taken to secure the latest editions. The reason is so obvious in such subjects as biology, physics, electricity and even mathematics, that it is unnecessary to do more than to state the principle. Text books and school editions should be provided with discrimination, as children can really benefit from them only by possessing them. Translations, cribs, keys to books of mathematics, etc., should not be provided at all; again for obvious school reasons.

While the latest edition of recognized books should as a rule be got, we should not be in too great a hurry to acquire the newest treatise; it is not necessarily better than an earlier one. It is better to have enough copies of a really good book to meet all demands than to buy individual copies of several inferior books. This is particularly true of classic fiction, of which it is not too much to say that there should be enough copies to meet every immediate demand and for a copy in excess always to be on the shelves. Clearly only experience and the circumstances of the individual library can determine what the number of copies shall be.

4

A part of the librarian's equipment is to know children's books; that is obvious enough, but is not so easy as may lightly be supposed. Many writers of good books have no fame in the ordinary literary world and their work can be overlooked. It is almost as important to know the publishers of children's books, and a postcard will bring their catalogues. The best librarians have a rough-and-ready mental classification of publishers which connects Blackie with the Henty, Fenn, Westerman type of book; Sampson Low with Kingston, others of Henty, Jules Verne and so on. Do not neglect American publishers.

5

Now-a-days many children read simple books in foreign languages. In America this would seem a commonplace, as there are problems of foreign immigrant populations which touch us, and then very slightly, only at our great seaports. A few books in French, German, Italian and Spanish are worth trying in the library.

6

I am unable to give with any accuracy a statement of the cost of children's books, but taking an average of a thousand books recently added to a junior library, I find the cost per volume to have been 3s. 7d. gross. This will do as a working factor for new books, but second-hand books will cost less and out-of-print books, on the rare occasions when it is thought necessary to have them, will cost more. American books are somewhat more costly than British, and for foreign books no average can be given as this must depend upon exchange rates. For ordinary English books a discount of 10 per cent. on the published price should be received.

7

The simplest means of recording book suggestions is to write them on cartridge slips (5 in. by 3 in.) ruled like the standard catalogue card. These slips can be obtained from any library supplier. The slip should bear the name of the author, title, publisher and price and an indication of the source of the suggestion. The date of order is stamped on this slip, which while the order remains unfilled is placed in an ordinary card tray or drawer behind a guide bearing the name of the bookseller. When the book is supplied the date of its arrival is stamped on the slip. Re-orderings or alterations should be clearly recorded in ink. These slips when completed can be filed in alphabetical order and to form a current catalogue of accessions. If several copies of a book are ordered from different booksellers a slip must be made out for each book with the number of copies clearly shown. I give a sample of such a slip:—

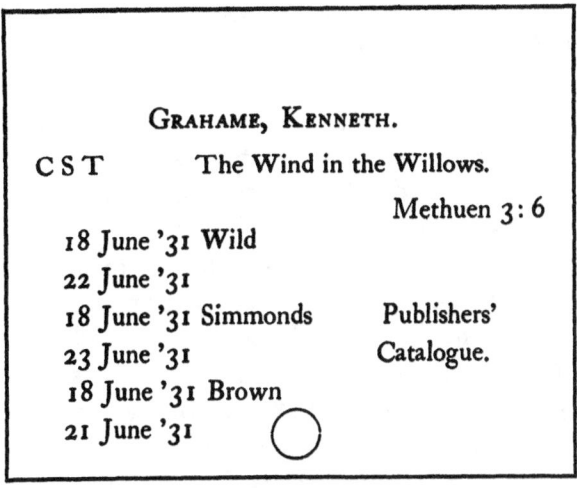

ORDER SLIP

The letters, CST, indicate the three libraries for which copies are wanted. A copy was ordered from each of three booksellers, Wild, Simmonds, and Brown, on the 18th of June, and the second date in each case is that of its receipt.

In ordering the book the list should state its particulars fully, in typewritten form preferably, and a duplicate copy should of course be kept for checking purposes.

BOOK SELECTION AND ACCESSION

8

These methods do not dispense with one indispensable course wherever it is possible: *All children's books should be obtained on approval in the first place.* This can easily be arranged in the ordinary town and most booksellers are willing to send books for examination. In fact, examination is the only means by which a sound selection can be made in all of our classes. Catalogues, reviews and announcements often omit indispensable information as to size, type, paper illustration and even literary form, as we have seen. In some libraries all books are read and in doubtful cases discussed by the staff. This cannot always be done, but rapid examination will generally tell an experienced librarian whether a book will do or not. Large libraries usually arrange with an agent that every child's book that is published shall be sent for examination, and where this can be done it is the best possible practice.

9

After receipt the books are cut, stamped, classified and catalogued and the charging cards mentioned in Chapter VIII are written for them. All books are entered into a stock book, or as it is commonly called an Accessions Book, which is ruled as follows and forms the inventory of the library. A simple ruling as follows serves for this, but standard rulings can be obtained from libraries or the Library Bureau.

A MANUAL OF CHILDREN'S LIBRARIES

Date	No.	Author	Title	Publisher	Price	Vendor	Condition	Class	Remarks

RULING FOR A CHILDREN'S LIBRARY'S ACCESSIONS BOOK

BOOK SELECTION AND ACCESSION

GUIDES TO BOOK SELECTION

Current Books

THE PUBLISHERS' CIRCULAR (weekly).
 (This with its annual cumulation, called *The English Catalogue*, gives a list of every book published with particulars of publisher and price.)

THE PUBLISHERS' WEEKLY.
 (A similar American list.)

THE BOOKSELLER.
 (An alternative as a list of new publications to *The Publishers' Circular*.)

"THE TIMES" EDUCATIONAL and LITERARY SUPPLEMENTS (weekly).

WHITAKER. Reference Catalogue of Current Literature. (A combination of all publishers' catalogues with an invaluable index, produced every few years.)

AMERICAN LIBRARY ASSOCIATION.
 Book list: a guide to new books (monthly). (A classified, annotated and indexed list with further selections for small libraries.)
 Children's Library Year Book, 1928—(Gives a list of the best American books of the year).

LIBRARY ASSOCIATION. Books to Read: a classified and annotated catalogue, being a guide for young readers. 1930. (For adolescent readers mainly. Supplements are issued.)

FIELD, W. T. A Guide to Literature for Children. 1928. N.Y.: Ginn.

KERNAHAN, COULSON. The Reading Girl. 1925. Harrap.

OLCOTT, F. J. The Children's Reading. 1912. Boston: Houghton Mifflin Co.

POTTER, M. E., and Others. Children's Catalogue: a guide to the best reading for young people. 1909. Supplement to 1919 by Corenne Bacon. 1919. *Standard Catalogues.* N.Y.: Wilson.

A MANUAL OF CHILDREN'S LIBRARIES

STEVENSON, LILIAN. A Child's Bookshelf. 1922.
Student Christian Movement.
(Useful for the tinies.)

WILLISON, MARJORY. Golden Treasury of Famous Books: a guide for boys and girls and for those who love books. 1929. Toronto: Macmillan.

WINNETKA Graded Book List. Results of a statistical investigation as to books enjoyed by children of various ages and measured degrees of reading ability. By Carleton Washburne and Mabel Vogel. 1926. Chicago: American Library Association.

Useful catalogues, issued by the Public Libraries named, which may be consulted to advantage are:

Bethnal Green. What Shall I Read? A catalogue of books in the Children's Library. 1930.

Glasgow. Woodside Branch. Guide for Young Readers. 1921.

St. Marylebone, London. Catalogue and Guide to the Books in the Children's Department. 1927.

Sheffield. One Thousand and One Best Books for Boys and Girls. 1930.

Toronto. Books for Boys and Girls: two thousand books which the librarians of the boys and girls division deem to be of definite and permanent interest: with annotations and descriptions. 1927.

AUTHORITIES

BASCOM, E. L. Book Selection. A.L.A. Manual of Library Economy, No. XVI. 1925. Chicago: A.L.A.

BROWN, J. D., Manual of Library Economy. Chap. XIII—Book Selection. 1931. Grafton.

McCOLVIN, L. R. Theory of Book Selection.
(As its title implies, this is a purely theoretical work. It is interesting as a brave attempt to find a philosophy of book-selection.)

BOOK SELECTION AND ACCESSION

POWELL, S. H. The Children's Library. Chap. 9—Book selection. 1917. N.Y.: Wilson Co.

SAWYER, H. P. The Library and Its Contents. Pp. 109–168, —Book Selection: children's literature. 1925. N.Y.: Wilson Co.

For accession methods, see Brown's *Manual* and any other general text books of library economy, and Hopper and Cannon's pamphlet, *Order and Accessions Department*, 1926, which is one of the chapters, to be obtained separately of the *A.L.A. Manual of Library Economy* (Chicago: A.L.A.)

CHAPTER V

THE CARE OF BOOKS

I

From the day the book enters the library its care is a matter of concern to the librarian. It is "collated" on its arrival to see that it is complete; that all the "signatures" are present. Signatures are the letters of the alphabet (or sometimes numbers) which are used to mark the sections of which the book is composed. A section may consist of 8, 16, 32 or other number of pages according to the size of paper or the character of the press that has been used in printing it; but the most usual number is 16. At the beginning of each section the letter will be found, at the foot of the page as a rule, A marking pages 1–16, B pages 17–32 and so on. Accidents occasionally occur at the binders by which sections are sometimes omitted, duplicated or placed in wrong order. The illustrations should also be checked with the list at the beginning. In busy libraries these precautions are sometimes omitted on the ground that the first reader will discover the imperfection and that publishers never refuse to remedy it; but this appears to me to be a counsel of inefficiency, and in actual practice readers do not always point out the imperfections.

THE CARE OF BOOKS

2

Then the greatest care should be used in all the processes through which a book goes before it is ready for circulation. In some cases, fortunately fewer than a few years ago, the leaves must be cut. A flat, thin bone paper-knife with a true edge is the best tool for cutting such leaves; and the cutting of the tops of the leaves should be carried right to the back of each fold, otherwise when the book is opened the pages tear downwards at the back in an ugly manner. Irretrievable damage is sometimes done by the way in which identification stamps, labels and book-plates are inserted. Stamping that is indelible has not been discovered, and an ordinary aniline dye ink impressed with a rubber stamp is good enough for most purposes. The stamp should be tried on a clean piece of paper before being applied to the book in order that superfluous ink, which will smudge, may be avoided. If the book is stamped at consistent intervals, say of every 50 pages (i.e. pages 1, 51, 101, 201, etc.), at the beginning and end of the printed matter, and on the back of every whole-page illustration, this will be ample, and will show quite clearly to the experienced eye if any attempt has been made to erase the stamps. In some libraries steel stamps, like those used for cancelling postage stamps in the post office, are employed with printing ink; but these are difficult to use without offsetting. Valuable books are often marked by perforating stamps, which are in effect a set of minute punches cutting out the letters in the paper, but few children's libraries are likely to have many such books. All that is needed is some means of identifying the book.

3

Book-plates are inserted on the inside of the front cover. These can be well designed and artistic or are more usually merely labels bearing an abstract of the principal rules of the library. The following is an example of the severer sort; but there is no reason why something more beautiful cannot be contrived.

The pasting in of such a label is a simple matter, which, however, is often done badly. The label should be laid flat face downwards on a clean piece of paper, held firmly in the centre by the middle finger of the left hand, and the paste spread evenly over it, with especial attention to the edges. When fixed in the book a clean piece of blotting paper should be placed over it and it should be rubbed flat with a cloth or paper-knife. On the first fly-leaf should be pasted the date label in some such form as the example shown. This, unlike the book-plate, is tipped in with paste only by its left edge, so that it can be removed easily when it has been filled. Here the best method is to lay the label on its back, and to put over it a clean sheet of paper, so placed as to leave exposed only the edge to be pasted. The pasting will then be confined to that edge and will

THE CARE OF BOOKS

NORTHFIELD PUBLIC LIBRARIES

THE JUNIOR LIBRARY
(For Boys and Girls of School Age.)

No.........................   *Class No.*........................

1. **Hours: Central:** Mondays, Tuesdays, Thursdays and Fridays, 12 noon to 2 p.m., and 4 p.m. to 7 p.m. Wednesdays, 12 noon to 2 p.m., and 5 p.m. to 7 p.m. Saturdays, 11 a.m. to 1 p.m., and 2.30 p.m. to 5.30 p.m.

2. This book is to be returned on or before the date last marked on the date label. There will be a FINE of ONE PENNY a week, or part of a week, for all time it is kept after that date. It cannot be changed on the same day that it is borrowed.

3. You have promised to take great care of this book. Wrap it up in wet weather; use it with clean hands; do not turn down the leaves; keep it clean. You must pay for any damage it receives while it is in your possession.

4. *Should any infectious illness occur in your house, do not return this book to the Library, but send to inform the Medical Officer of Health at the Town Hall, who will tell you what to do. THIS IS MOST IMPORTANT.*

5. Should you change your address, report it to the Librarian at once.

not trickle over other parts of the label and so make it stick to the opposite page or cover.

> **Fifteen Days** (including days of issue and return) are allowed for reading. A fine of **One Penny per week or part of week** will be charged if it is kept longer. **Change of your address** should be notified immediately.
>
> **This book is due for return on or before the date last marked below.**

4

New books are usually published with paper "jackets" having a vividly attractive illustration upon them; and sometimes a brief note—called hideously a "blurb"—which purports to describe the story, albeit not always impartially. These may be removed and saved for exhibition on the library notice boards or screens as pointers to the additions. Some librarians prefer to issue the books to their readers with the jackets on, but one issue is usually fatal to a jacket. Others cut out the pictorial part of the jacket and paste it as an extra illustration into the books. Yet others save the jacket and when the book has been bound in library binding paste it on to the front board and varnish it; this makes books very attractive for a time, but the picture gets dirty with use.

5

Wear soon shows itself in the books; young fingers are proverbially more destructive than older ones. To give lessons in the care of books is an essential task of the children's librarian. They can be taught interestingly how to open a new book, in the manner described by the late Cedric Chivers in *The Library*,[1] who may be paraphrased. A new book should be held with both hands, each hand holding one of the boards firmly between the first and second finger; each thumb then opens about sixteen pages on each side and draws them tightly towards the board where the first finger takes them and presses them to it; the thumbs continue to take groups of about sixteen leaves and in the same manner draw them

[1] Second ser., Vol. I, p. 323, 1900.

Showing How to Open a Library Book

to the respective boards, at each movement forcing the boards gently a little further back. When the centre of the book is reached it is closed and the process is repeated. If it has been done properly the roundness of the back will be preserved, the sewing will not be broken, and the book will open easily and remain open.

The librarian will require readers to have clean hands from the outset, and must not depart from this requirement; sentiment must not allow the property of the library to be damaged, and lessons, individual or to classes in such matters as the effect of dirt on paper; the ill-results that occur to books and may occur to readers of the wetting of fingers when turning leaves; the destructiveness of rain, of reading a book too near a warm fire, of wrestling with it physically as well as mentally, of using it as a weapon of offence or defence; or as a stand for hot teapots, jugs or cups; the undesirability of allowing dogs to practice their masticating powers upon it—these and many other subjects of like character should be inculcated almost as carefully as should be the methods of extracting knowledge from books. Some libraries, where a bookbinder is employed, get him to demonstrate many of these points to children; but usually it must be done by the librarian. Sometimes brief lectures on book care are given as a preface to ordinary library talks or lectures. An exhibition of books which have suffered different sorts of damage with labels on causes and their avoidance has had good results or has at least drawn attention to these troubles. With children the librarian should absolutely *insist* upon the sense of responsibility being exercised.

6

When damage, either by use or abuse, occurs it should be made good, if possible without delay. This leads us to the subject of the binding and repair of books. A few first principles are that the librarian should know enough of the craft of bookmaking and binding to be able to recognize good workmanship so as to be able to command it; that such repairs as are undertaken in the library itself should be of the most elementary sort, since a clumsy repair may do damage that cannot be rectified; that readers should never be allowed to repair books, as their faith in the virtues of stamp-edging for mending torn pages is fervid, and their use of paste or glue reckless. Books with many loose leaves, torn cases, or broken sewing are matter for the professional binder; economy requires that they go to him. In the cases of leaves slightly torn, or slightly stained, or loose plates, the librarian can effect temporary repair.

For such repair a few tools are needed, which should be good and are not costly. These may be set out:—

A sheet of thick plate glass for use as a slab on which paper or cardboard may be cut.
Cardboard knives.

Scissors.
Rulers with a hard true edge.
Strong linen thread.
Brushes for paste and glue: use a different brush for every medium.
Gluepot, which must be kept partly filled with water in order that it does not dry and crack.
A bone paper-knife ("folder").
Glue.
Paste of a good make; any book of trade recipes will give a method for making it, but most stationers have satisfactory brands.
Onion-skin paper.
Erasers.
A letter press is most useful if it can be obtained.

These will do to go on with, but the reader would be well advised to consult the trade catalogues of such firms as Gaylord Brothers, who are represented in England by the Woolston Company, Nottingham, of Libraco, Grafton and other library suppliers for repairing materials which have been found to be satisfactory.

Torn leaves should be laid flat on the glass slab, the torn edges drawn together so that they fit exactly; paste should be applied to the tear, very thinly, and a piece of tissue paper is then laid over it, and rubbed down gently with the folder. The book can be placed in the press until the leaf is quite dry. Then the tissue paper can be torn lightly and carefully away and it will be found that enough of it has adhered to the torn edges to make a neat and usually sufficient repair. In the case of heavy papers that would break from tissue papers, onion-

THE CARE OF BOOKS

skin or a transparent repairing tape—as made by one of the firms mentioned—should be used.

Single leaves or plates that have sprung are the commonest trouble of the librarian. The loose leaf is the more serious as it means that the opposite leaf in the signature of the book is also in danger of coming away, and that second leaf must be secured as well. Here the leaf should be laid on the slab, the edge to be pasted should be rubbed flat with the folder to remove uneven particles, and the page should be covered with a sheet of paper so as to leave exposed the edge to be pasted. Use only the thinnest application of paste, and fit the leaf into the book with meticulous care. The same process should be used for loose plates. In both cases remember that too much paste may do great damage.

There are really few other repairs that can be made satisfactorily by the librarian who is not a skilled binder. Occasionally a signature of a book comes away, and this can be sewn in, but as the whole of the sewing of a book is interdependent, when one signature comes away the others will soon follow. However, if the book has an open-back, that is, if the case is not fastened to the back of the book, it is possible to re-sew a section by passing the needle through the middle of the signature from the inside, letting it fall down the inside of the open back and catching and passing it into the signature again, tying on to the end of the thread left when the needle started the operation. But it is better to leave this job to the binder.

Tea and coffee stains can sometimes be removed by applying a lather of soap to the stain and rinsing and drying. Jam stains require a solution of soap and a little carbonate of soda in warm water which should be sponged gently over the stain, and rinsing and drying in clean water follows. Ink, which is a bug-bear of library life, can be removed (with difficulty) in two or three ways, but perhaps the best, albeit the slowest, is to place blotting-paper under the sheet, moisten the stain with lemon juice and then dab with a pad of clean white rag, and to keep repeating lemon juice and dabbing until all the ink is removed. Mud can be removed by washing the page with a soapy solution and rinsing and drying afterwards. Grease or oil is most simply dealt with by placing clean white blotting-paper over the place affected and ironing with a hot, but not too hot, flat iron. Change the paper several times and keep the iron hot. The paper will absorb the stain completely as a rule in a few applications. Pencil marks and many ordinary dust stains can be removed by a rubber eraser, but it must be used gently so as not to rub away the tissues of the paper. Some papers, of course, are so frail that they disintegrate under even gentle rubbing.

7

When a book comes whole out of its case, it may be "re-cased" by a binder, but the vile method of pasting on the cover again, which was sometimes practised, should be avoided, as it means that the paste, nearly always applied too thickly, will rot the backs of the sections and make permanent binding difficult if not impossible at a later stage. Early binding is sound library economy. So much is this so that many modern libraries do not circulate books if they can help it in publishers' cases at all. They get a professional binder, who specializes in work for libraries, to obtain them in sheets from the publishers and to bind them first and finally in a library binding before they are brought into use. This has several advantages. It makes unnecessary most of the repairs that occupy our time, as these are usually the result of the defective sewing which is frequently due to commercial machine case making; and the books when once in circulation have not to be withdrawn for binding and so the time wasted in preparing books for the binders is saved, and readers have the uninterrupted use of them until they are worn out. The recent efforts of binders to produce decorative bindings have removed part of the objection to this method. That objection is that a new book in a publisher's cover is far more attractive to the average reader than any permanent library binding. Opinion is divided on the matter, and it is difficult to say whether or not this objection applies to children's books; my own observations in the matter have been somewhat negative in results.

A MANUAL OF CHILDREN'S LIBRARIES

AUTHORITIES

AMERICAN LIBRARY ASSOCIATION. Committee on Bookbinding. Care and Binding of Books. 1928. Chicago: A.L.A.

BROWN, M. W. Mending and Repair of Books. 1921. Chicago: A.L.A.

CHIVERS, CEDRIC. How to Open a New Book. *In* the Library, 1900, pp. 323–26.
(Has 10 illustrations of the process recommended.)

COUTTS, H. T., and STEPHEN, G. A. Manual of Library Bookbindings: practical and historical. Illus. 1911.
(Chapter X deals with book-repairing.)

CHAPTER VI

BOOKBINDING

I

The ordinary librarianship studies include a course on library bookbinding, but it is only in small and not very busy libraries that the librarian can do actual binding of books. Library binding is now a specialized occupation, and its materials and processes have been so worked upon that good-looking bindings which are strong enough to outlast the books themselves can be obtained at a reasonable cost. This cost may be assessed in a general way as about one-third of the original value of the volume to be bound, but this figure is subject to all sorts of variations.

The children's librarian will not require a comprehensive knowledge of binding, but will necessarily be the more efficient for possessing it. What must be known are the right materials for different types of book, the nature of the sewing, and ability to assess the finishing work which consists of the tooling, lettering and other decoration employed by the binder is highly desirable. The following simple principles are worth study:—

1. A book should be bound when its case is torn, when its tapes have been broken so that they cannot be replaced on the boards, when its sewing has broken, or when the leaves begin to come out.

2. When original cases have been so handled that the title and author, sometimes merely printed lightly on covers, have become indecipherable, they should be sent to the binder for re-lettering, if the case will bear it, or be re-bound if it will not.
3. Books which have lost a few pages or a plate can sometimes be completed at a small cost if application is made to the publishers.
4. A book which has such narrow inner margins that the binder cannot sew the leaves without obscuring the text should be discarded.
5. Books which have papers light in texture, and books which are rarely handled, should be bound in cloth.
6. Books with heavy papers, art or semi-art papers, and most books which are subjected to much use should be bound in half or quarter leather. Leather requires a certain amount of grease to keep it in condition, and this the natural oil from our hands supplies in ordinary use.

2

A book is said to be *whole-bound* when it is covered entirely in one kind of material, but leather is generally meant. It is *three-quarters bound* when it has a wide strip of leather at the back and the sides are covered with cloth; and *half-bound* when a narrower strip is used. Both three-quarter and half-bound books have leather over the corners. A *quarter bound* book has a still narrower leather back. For ordinary purposes half-binding is quite suitable and usual, but quarter-binding is good enough for many books, especially cheap ones.

On the sewing used by the binder the strength of the book depends. Books with sections so broken that many of the leaves are separate can be oversewn, a method which gives strength and, if well done, is quite satisfactory. Some librarians do not like it and affirm that a book which is overcast from the back will not open easily, but so long as the method is applied only to books with good inner margins it is stronger than and is as convenient as any method. The other methods are those which sew the sections as units to each other, known as *sewing all-along* and *sewing "two on."* In this method the binder usually reinforces every fold with thin, tough paper guards, and it gives a strong book which lies flat when open. The book is sewn on to strong linen tapes, the ends of which are glued on to the boards, or, more often nowadays, the boards are split at the edges and the tapes are firmly inserted. Four tapes are usual in a well-bound crown-octavo.

3

When books require to be bound, they should be carefully collated to see that they are perfect, and when not an effort should be made to supply the missing parts. A list of the books should accompany each batch of binding with instructions as to the lettering, and sometimes the actual treatment of individual books. A sheet with ruling as follows is satisfactory, and, of course, it should be made in duplicate so that the librarian retains a copy of the exact instructions sent:—

A MANUAL OF CHILDREN'S LIBRARIES

No.	Date when sent	Author	Title	Class-mark	Material	Style	Colour	Date returned
2	4 June, 1931	Hudson	Afoot in England	828	Niger	‡	Green	24 June, 1931

BOOKBINDING

Some librarians place a slip in each book, as follows:—

```
CROYDON PUBLIC LIBRARIES

Central        No. 11173

Style_____    Colour_____

Price_____    Binder_____

Outside height must not exceed
9⅞-in.    11⅞-in.    15¾-in.
```

Send Accounts in Duplicate, and quote binding numbers only, not authors nor titles.
Return in binding no. sequences.

When books are returned they should be accompanied by an invoice, but it is obvious that they should be checked carefully to see that the batch is complete and that the work has been done aright. Errors should always be returned for correction.

The children's librarian will wisely prefer well-decorated bindings, as these attract. Especially is this to be remembered when rebinding the classics; an attractive cover has often been the means of introducing a great work to a child, and such aids are not to be despised.

4

This is hardly the place for a discussion of binding materials, but it may be said that morocco and niger leathers are usual and are best for ordinary books which are to be well used. Pigskin is heavy, tough and durable, and is to be preferred for heavy books on loaded papers. A good washable cloth—Winterbottom's, for example—is suitable for many kinds of less used and very cheap books which will not bear a leather case. Calf and roan are delicate, and these as well as the split roan called skiver (or, indeed, any split leather) should be avoided, while vellum, that white and attractive hard leather, is so difficult to handle that it is not to be recommended.

When the librarian has not acquired any technical knowledge of binding a specialist firm should be called in to do the work in the most suitable way. Some of these firms have an excellent record not only for past work but also for continuous effort at securing more efficient and attractive work. A mass of valuable information will be found in the

BOOKBINDING

books listed at the end of this chapter, and the librarian may be assured that knowledge of binding and its possibilities will effect many economies and do much to keep the library stock bright and alluring.

AUTHORITIES

BAILEY, A. L. Library Bookbinding. 1916. N.Y.: Wilson Co.

BROWN, J. D. Manual of Library Economy. Chap. 22—Bookbinding and Repairing. 1931. Grafton.
(Gives a full specification, and has diagrams of methods of lettering.)

COCKERELL, DOUGLAS. Bookbinding and the Care of Books: a textbook for bookbinders and librarians. 1901. John Hogg.

—— Some Notes on Bookbinding. 1929. Oxford University Press.

HULME, E. W., and Others. Leather for Libraries. 1905. Libraco.

PHILIP, A. J. The Business of Bookbinding. 1912. Stanley Paul.

PART II
THE CHILDREN'S LIBRARY

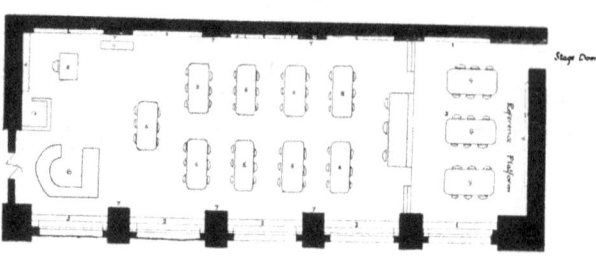

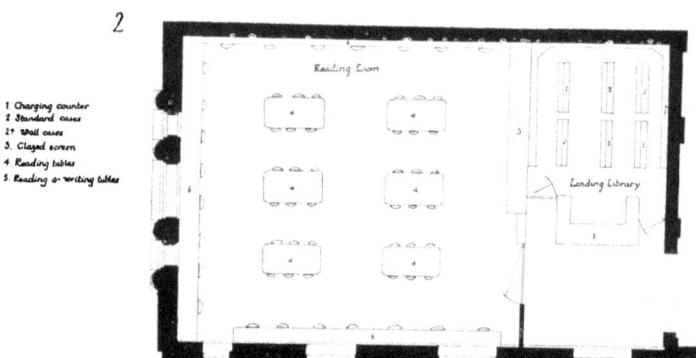

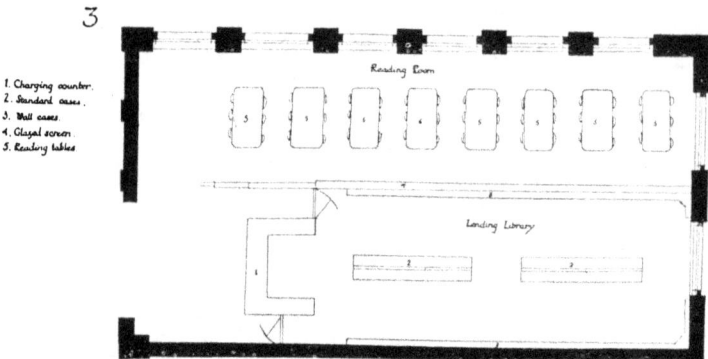

PLANS OF CHILDREN'S LIBRARIES
1. In a room divided only by furniture.
2. With a separate apartment for the Lending Library (on the Islington Plan).
3. With a glazed barrier dividing Lending and Reading Departments.

Drawn by Eva K. West

CHAPTER VII

MAKING THE CHILDREN'S LIBRARY

I

Having studied what a child reads let us now consider what has been done in England to provide reading matter for the child. As the book for the child was the most recent form of English literature, so the most recent form of library provision has been for children.

To some extent their claims were recognized all along. In her interesting book called *Libraries for Children*, which is the most comprehensive account of actual work done, Miss Gwendolen Rees has traced briefly the growth of libraries for the young in England. Pioneer work was done by the Mechanics' Institute. Children who could afford a penny could borrow a book from the Mechanics' Institute at Birmingham in 1797, and these Mechanics' Institutes were to a large extent the forerunners of the public libraries—that is to say, the municipal libraries—of this country. But I agree with Miss Rees that probably the bulk of the children in England were served for the first half of the nineteenth century by the books published by the Religious Tract Society, which were issued to them through their Sunday schools. Other books went to make these Sunday school libraries besides these definitely religious publications of the Religious Tract Society.

2

Most of the books dealt with in our first chapter were produced for well-to-do children, but in the first half of the nineteenth century even they had no very wide access to books, because we have seen that sufficient books did not exist. As for library provision for other children: Miss Rees remarks that these Sunday school libraries have ceased to exist for the most part, but I think there are still many villages in England where they play a really important part in the life of the child, and it is quite legitimate to expect that religious teaching should be given to children through their means. The Sunday school libraries of my own youth were not very attractive affairs; the books were clothed in a drab cloth of uniform dinginess, and the title was written on a draper's label stuck on to the back. But amongst these books I have found the works of Henty, Fenn, A.L.O.E. and one or two other writers not to be found elsewhere in the country town of which I am speaking.

A few words may be said on this question of the Sunday school library, because the probability is that professional librarians here and there may be called on to advise about such libraries. I believe such libraries are good things; but I believe they have been badly managed in the past. They have

MAKING THE CHILDREN'S LIBRARY

consisted of the off-scourings of other people's collections. The piety of some people has not always enabled them to see that the books which are too uninteresting for themselves to read and, therefore, books with which they could most easily dispense, are not likely to be of any particular value in the libraries where they bestow them. But a collection of books, religious or otherwise, chosen with deliberation, and graded to suit the needs of the various children attending Sunday schools, might be made a valuable auxiliary of the ordinary school or public library. The only rule that we should lay down here is that the books should be the best of their kind, and a book is not a good book because it mentions God, and tells the story of a man who is drowned because he goes to Brighton on a Sunday. So-called religious books are frequently most unchristian, irreligious and immoral.

That warning was by way of an aside. To proceed with our history. Ordinary day school libraries were established by the School Board of London in 1878. These were something like the school libraries we have now in several towns; that is to say, a collection of books was placed in each school and these were exchanged every six months. This provision did not extend to secondary schools which, however, seemed to have their stationary collections. We shall come back to this question of the school libraries when we come to consider, as we shall do later, the modern centralized school library system.

3

Usually the public library from its beginning recognized that it had a duty towards the child, but that was to be performed when every other interest had been adequately served. It is true that there was a Children's Room at Manchester in 1861—that is ten years after the passing of the first Public Libraries Act—but if my information is correct this was an underground room with no furniture but a long table and some school forms without backs, it being the general theory that a form, as it was an extremely awkward thing to sit upon and made the body uncomfortable, therefore made the mind more alert. A janitor in uniform stood at the door to inspect the hands of the incoming children; there were no books in the room—at least none were visible—these were handed over a counter by a somewhat forbidding person to the children who dared to apply for them. The main thing was to keep the little wretches quiet, and to hope in some way that they received improvement by the library attendance.

Miss Rees records that 743 children's books were issued from the Birkenhead Public Library in 1865. In 1882 the late Mr. J. Potter Briscoe made an interesting experiment at Nottingham in the provision of a separate Children's Lending Library. That is the whole story of the separate library provision for children until we reach the end of the nineteenth century.

MAKING THE CHILDREN'S LIBRARY

The usual method, however, was a few shelves, an alcove or an even somewhat larger space in the adult lending department; but until quite recently although the books were there they were limited to children who had reached the age of fourteen, save in exceptional circumstances. Nor was any fuller provision, much as librarians desired it, possible in the very limited financial circumstances of the public libraries of this country. Why this was so a glance at public library history makes quite clear; until 1919 the whole of the public libraries, except in one or two great cities which had special local acts of Parliament, had to be conducted upon the produce of a one-penny rate, which at its maximum meant something like sixpence yearly per head of the population. It was utterly out of the question under the old "penny rate system" to provide any adequate library on behalf of the child.

4

But in the nineties we came to realize that what was being done was gravely inadequate. In America, where the means of libraries were more generous, the library world appears to have arrived at a similar conclusion at much about the same time. It is often supposed that Americans have always had wonderful, well-staffed, adequate children's libraries. To-day they have; but forty years ago their position in this matter was not so very much better than our own. "In the summer of 1885" (I am quoting now from a paper by Miss Emily S. Hanaway in the *Library Journal*, May, 1887, reprinted in Hazeltine's *Library Work with Children*—a book I would commend), "while seated in a room where the National Association of Teachers had assembled, a thought, as if some one had leaned over my shoulder and suggested it, came suddenly into my mind: 'Why not give the children reading-rooms?' There was no getting rid of the thought. After the meeting, in the evening, I asked Professor E. E. White, of Ohio, if he thought such an undertaking could be carried out. He answered, 'yes; but it is gigantic.' " So we see where the Americans were half-way through the eighties—not so far ahead as we were in Manchester and Nottingham—they had no children's reading rooms at all, and the very notion of them came as a veritable inspiration to the lady I have quoted.

Meanwhile, some tentative efforts were made by English public libraries to solve the problem. Bootle, in 1894, produced a *Catalogue of Books for the Young*; every pupil in the schools was provided with a borrower's card; the youngsters chose books from the catalogue, and these were conveyed to the school in a hand-cart very like a postman's barrow. A somewhat primitive method, perhaps, but one which in the thirty years or more for which it has existed has done work of no mean quantity and quality.

MAKING THE CHILDREN'S LIBRARY

5

Of all the experiments those at Cardiff were the most effective. Here there grew up the idea of a *whole* library service for the child; and it consisted of a combination of reading halls at the branch libraries and of rotating lending collections at the schools. Almost contemporary with those libraries were those which were in vogue in London for many years. At Cable Street, Stepney, in one of the poorest and most forlorn quarters of London, my own attention was first drawn to the children's library in 1904. Here was a room actually set aside for children. It had books and reading tables in it. It was not specially beautiful, but the seeds of the thing were there. The books were visible to the children in cases around the walls of the room, but they could be handled only by the library staff: the bookcases being covered with an iron grill.

There was a somewhat similar room for children in the very different borough of Chelsea; and in both of these libraries the books could be seen and called for; but could not be taken from the shelves by the children themselves.

It will be seen that in these libraries was something which a librarian with any imagination could certainly adapt. John Ballinger at Cardiff went far beyond them. His rooms for children were—as I have already shown in their name—halls, of equal dignity with any other apartment—in fact, better than any other apartment in the libraries in which

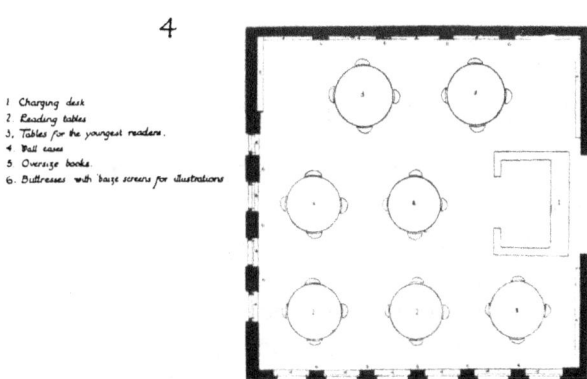
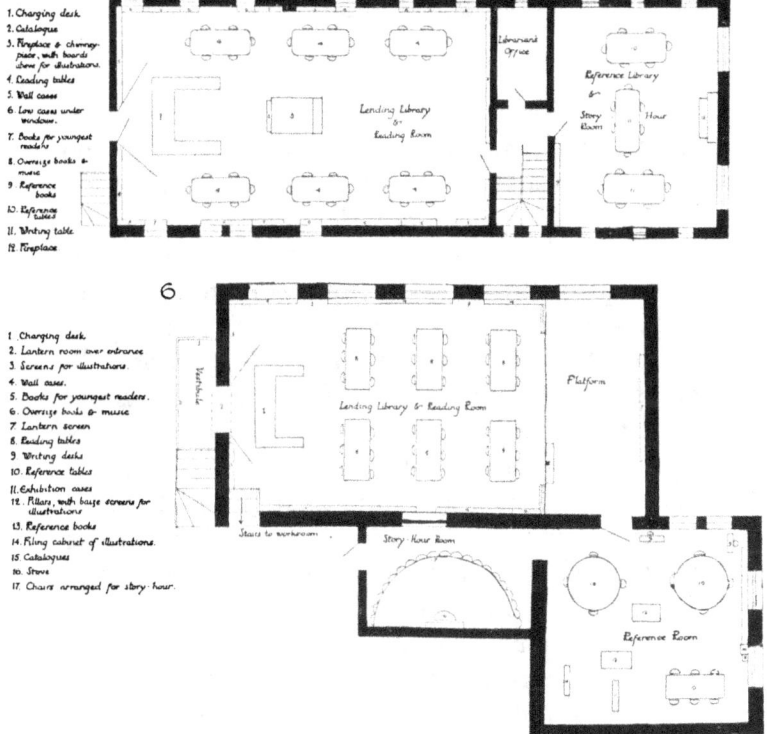

PLANS OF CHILDREN'S LIBRARIES
4. With all activities in one square room.
5. With a special room for Reference Work and Story-Telling.
6. In a very busy area, with separate Reference and Story-Telling Rooms.

Drawn by Eva K. West

they were situated. They were lofty, well-lighted and ventilated; they were decorated with pictures; they were in the care of a member of the staff who was devoted solely to the needs of the youngsters. But they were reading and reference libraries only; the books could be read in the room, but could not be taken to their homes by the children. This need of a book to read at home was met by a collection in the adult lending libraries; and by a pioneer system of rotating school libraries.

6

This was the history, speaking generally but by no means exhaustively, of the library movement for children in England until the Islington Libraries were opened in about 1906, when James Duff Brown provided a system of children's libraries which were in effect a service parallel in nearly all the facilities offered with the adult libraries. In parenthesis, we may say that it should be realized that in the average population, other than in the very centres of large towns where people do not *live*, the children of reading age form at least one-third of the total population. Moreover, the youngsters are greater readers both actually and potentially than adults, and a much greater proportion of the resources of a municipal library ought to be devoted to them than is anywhere the case yet. Brown at Islington introduced one of the standard forms of the planning of a children's library which still

MAKING THE CHILDREN'S LIBRARY

obtain. The whole department was in a large room. In the centre of the room were tables on which were children's periodicals; along the walls were desks equipped with pens and ink where they could write; and in proximity to these were a few of the best reference books for their use—dictionaries, atlases, encyclopædias and similar works. About one-third of the room, near to the entrance, was screened off by a glass partition, making a small room. This was an open access lending library.

The criticism I have to make of the Islington system as it then existed was that there were no special children's assistants; the department was run by the ordinary library assistants in rota as part of their ordinary duties; but then James Duff Brown did not favour specialism in library work—the keynote of all library service to-day. However that may be, his libraries were so successful that the police had to be called to regulate the crowds of children who desired to enter them. This was a state that could not go on; and children were in time limited to certain days and hours in the week in their use of the libraries.

7

In 1920, after the War had so muddled library departments that newsrooms were still Food Control, Recruiting or other War emergency offices, I was afforded the opportunity at Croydon of working at the subject. I thought that the library ought to be the parallel matter that I have already mentioned.

A MANUAL OF CHILDREN'S LIBRARIES

A children's public library, rather than a mere children's department, was the ideal in mind. An adult library consists of reference library, lending library, periodicals room, lecture room, newspaper room, etc. Why not give the children all of these things? But, of course, no librarian ever has space to do that. I had one room only; it was 70 feet long. I could go back to an old system that I had seen in Amsterdam in 1912. I would make it beautiful, comfortable, comprehensive—if I could get the money. To my surprise I found that it was easier to get the money for anything for the children than it was for the grown-ups. An enthusiastic artist in the Borough Engineer's Department worked out my colour schemes for me.

Thus, then, my room. The walls were decorated up to 3 feet in Spanish red of a glossy character; then two deep green lines; then cream with a blush-rose pink in it. So we got an effect as utterly unofficial as we could. Bookcases to 4 feet 6 inches in height ran along the walls between buttresses; on the buttresses were framed green baize screens. On the walls were pictures of determined rank, some of local subjects but mainly legendary and literary pictures, as Watts's *Sir Galahad*, Holliday's *Meeting of Dante and Beatrice*, *The Boyhood of Drake*, and the historical panels from the House of Lords. All doors and windows were curtained. The little statuette, *The Winged Victory*, was placed in a corner.

The room was divided roughly into three parts, marked by their uses. It was a lecture-room, too.

MAKING THE CHILDREN'S LIBRARY

At the end farthest from the entrance we raised a platform, about 20 inches high. Behind this we had a lantern screen on the wall, which could be covered with a velvet curtain when not in use. At this platform end we put our reference books on either side and on the edge of the platform; and on the platform we put tables with seats for eighteen readers. Here could be done homework, authorship, or very quiet reading.

On the long walls of the room the cases contained the books which could be read in other parts of the room (if desired) or be borrowed for home reading. Throughout, the shelves were about 4 feet 6 inches in height; shelves in a children's library are wisely kept at less than 5 feet in height.

The centre of the room was filled with tables, having 6-foot gangways between them. The tables were about 2 inches lower than the ordinary dining-room table; and chairs were also lower in proportion. Other special points about the tables were that they were oblong, being 6 feet by 2 feet 9 inches, were rounded at each end, and they folded up if necessary. This last feature enabled them to be cleared away when it was desired to chair the room to its full capacity for lectures.

The series of plans which are reproduced will give some idea of the various types of library, and any librarian could easily adapt a room in accordance with some such plan, or by combining them. The most attractive plan is that of the Cardiff or Manchester library, which has a reference and reading room only, and has no lending library. In his *The Child as Reader*, L. Stanley Jast describes the theory of the work he has done at Manchester where the work is still in an experimental state. "It is hoped that some day the accommodation and the staff in Manchester will enable us to throw our rooms open without restriction, but the expense will be heavy," writes Mr. Jast. At present the Manchester library is a well-furnished, well-stocked and well-staffed reading room, to which children selected by teachers in the elementary schools are admitted by ticket. The point of the system is that by limiting the number the librarian is able to know the children personally, to teach them the right use of books, and to watch over their reading. All this is admirable, but it will occur to most readers that the system creates a privileged class of readers. It is not a public library for children, but a reading centre maintained by the municipality for children whom teachers think will best benefit by it. It could only be fair if Mr. Jast's ideal were realized of enough libraries for the whole child community to be treated in the individual fashion he describes. The argument is worth considering, however, that it is better to do well for a few children what might be done very badly if it were attempted for all.

The books which are required for home reading are supplied in Manchester through the ordinary adult lending libraries. This is also done at Cardiff where, in addition, there are the schools libraries already mentioned.

MAKING THE CHILDREN'S LIBRARY

This Manchester reading-and-reference type of library is that which should exist in every boarding school; for all I say in this book about method, with very few exceptions, can be made to apply to the school as well as to the public library for children. The potentialities in the school of a well-organized library under a trained librarian are far from being realized in this country; they are hardly even recognized.

8

The plans of a whole children's service are, it may be repeated, of two kinds; that where all the work is done in one large room in which the divisions are made by the character of the furniture and the books, but are otherwise invisible, as shown in plan No. 1, and a smaller simpler type in one room as is shown in plan 4; and that where the lending library is definitely screened off from the reading room, as in plan No. 2.

The first of these two (1) is the Croydon system, and the second (2) may be studied in the Walton Branch of the Liverpool Public Libraries or at the Islington Central Library. The large room makes every department a link in a single chain, but in some districts it is feared that the children will make too much noise in choosing books to allow reading to go on at the same time. In experience it has been found that while it is impossible to get absolute quiet in any children's room, and it ought not to be expected, "reasonable quiet"—as James D

Stewart wisely defined the requirements in his own excellent library at Bermondsey—can be obtained by proper supervision. The choice between the two systems, however, can well be left to the individual librarian.

Plan 3 shows the kind of lay-out existing in the children's libraries at Great Smith Street, Westminster, and at the Fulham Central Library. Two other plans are given: one (Fig. 6) of a library which uses three rooms, the largest one as the lending library with magazines on the centre tables, a somewhat smaller room as a children's study or reference library, and a third, and again smaller, room for story hours. This division is made in a very busy neighbourhood where the library is used by so many children that it seems desirable to be able to hold story hours and to give children quiet places for school homework at the time when lending library work and the reading of periodicals are going on. The second (Fig. 5) shows two rooms, the larger of which is lending library and periodicals rooms, and the smaller combines the purposes of a reference library and, when required, of story-hour room.

Plans for such libraries may be very elaborate with the special furniture described in the next chapter. On the other hand they may be very simple. While it is desirable to have a children's library with handsome shelves and beautiful furniture, with different sizes for the different ages of children, it would be a pity if any district waited for sufficient funds to reach all its ideals. A simple room distempered in bright colours with the plainest furniture and quite ordinary chairs is far better than nothing. To create a real children's library, books and a librarian are the main requirements. She will bring good taste in the way of simple, inexpensive accessories—good but cheap pictures, wild and garden flowers in their seasons to give physical beauty, and her own culture and leading to vitalize the room.

All of which means that excellent as are some of the libraries for children in their physical equipment, the librarian and her spirit are ultimately the main factors in making a successful children's library.

AUTHORITIES

BROWN, JAMES DUFF. Manual of Library Economy. Ed. 4. 1930. Grafton.

KING, WILLIAM A. The Elementary School Library. 1929. Scribner.

LANGSTAFF, JOHN BRETT. The David Copperfield Library 1924. Allen & Unwin.

THE HUNSLET JUNIOR LIBRARY, LEEDS
Photograph lent by the Leeds Public Libraries

CHAPTER VIII

THE EQUIPMENT OF THE LIBRARY

1

If our library is to be successful it must be in every way suitable for its purpose. In the last chapter some indications were given to show that the position of the room, its decoration and furniture and fittings were all designed to produce an atmosphere. The means may be simple or elaborate, but careful consideration should be given to every article so that the room may be healthy, attractive, and produce a feeling of respect for it on the part of its user. Old theory held that given space, a stool to sit upon and something to read the child was satisfied, but that theory has died of senility; and children react in no uncertain manner to neatness, beauty, in short, appropriateness in their surroundings. The equipment of a children's library is a valuable factor in producing the discipline without which it must be a failure. We want to make a room which will give to the child generally most of the characteristics of a private study.

2

The room should be the best that can be devoted to the purpose; basements, or top floors of high buildings, are sometimes used of necessity, but it

THE EQUIPMENT OF THE LIBRARY

is better to have a room on the ground floor. One approached by stairs, either up or down, has the objection that accidents may occur, and in this connexion it should be remembered that libraries are responsible for accidents to children which happen in this way; the child under age cannot, in the eyes of the law, contribute to its own injury. When, therefore, stairs are unavoidable such possibilities must be foreseen. On this question it may be said that not only by the provision of proper handrails and other preventatives the library must be safeguarded, but insurances against financial liability for accidents must be undertaken as well. Part of the equipment of the library is, of course, a first-aid outfit, which can be obtained from any chemist, so that minor mishaps may be dealt with immediately.

3

Wherever the room is, proper lighting, heating and ventilation are essentials; the nature and quality of these must be determined by the place. A north light, so long as it is plentiful, is a good natural light because it does not permit direct sunlight upon the books, but opinion will naturally be in favour of a sunny room. Ideal artificial lighting is indirect lighting by electric light, but this is expensive, and semi-indirect lighting which uses a white ceiling for reflection purposes and if quite evenly distributed serves well. The artificial daylight known as "restlight" is probably the best now available. Every room is a separate lighting problem, and experiments should be made before a system is adopted. It is quite obvious, too, that if a room is used occasionally for lectures involving a lantern, suspended lights must not fall in the beam of the lantern. Again, lights should be low enough for the illumination to reach the vertical faces of the shelves to the bottom shelf, but should not be so low that they can be reached by readers.

Ventilation is rarely as satisfactory as it might be. In this respect it is like acoustics, and a successfully ventilated room often comes by good fortune rather than design. A frequent change of air, without draughts, is required. Where the ventilation is sluggish electric fans will give some assistance.

Heating is another matter well worth study. For comfort and cheerfulness an old-fashioned fireplace would be very nice, but open fires cannot be recommended in any public building, and are perhaps particularly dangerous in libraries. Usually heating will be by radiators supplied with hot water or steam. For medium-sized rooms, where there is no elaborate central heating system, heating by electricity can be very effective and attractive, especially by such electric fires as the magi-coal which can imitate realistically a real fire.

3

The treatment of the walls is worth careful planning. The position of the windows will determine where

THE EQUIPMENT OF THE LIBRARY

the bookcases are to go, and the presence of buttresses and the shape of the room also determine where the lantern screen, platform (if any), and screens for illustrations are to be placed. I have already described the colour scheme of one library, and I do not prescribe any scheme as suitable for all libraries. A white ceiling and light colours on the upper parts of the walls produce the maximum of light. In fairly sunny districts dark colours and dark furniture, if used with restraint, are not objectionable, but in our British climate the brighter the room the better. Mahogany scratches easily, and is not so desirable as the light fumed oak which is ordinarily used. Steel shelves, which can be obtained in almost any colour, are frequently used. One American librarian suggests a cream-coloured wall, furniture finished in pearly grey and a large bowl of orange or deep blue placed conspicuously somewhere in the room to lend a bright note of colour.

The walls should be portioned out. The best walls for shelves, and, indeed, for other purposes, are those which are exactly opposite windows. These should be shelved for the books that are most used, or which we desire to have most used. Shelves under windows are relatively dark but must often be used. There are many kinds of shelves in wood and in steel, and the firms specializing in library appliances are the best people to provide these. They should be movable or, as librarians say, adjustable; that is to say, be capable of movement so that the shelves can be made to take large or small books. The two best-known shelf fittings are called the Vernier and Tonks'. Shelves should not exceed 5 feet in height, and are better 6 inches lower. The lowest shelf should be at least a foot from the ground, and shelves should be 3 feet in length, and be 7 inches deep (from front to back), except for heavy books such as music, for which they should not exceed 18 inches in length, but must be 10 inches in depth. Part of the room should be given up to large books, and the shelves for these must be deeper; a length of about 12 inches and a depth of 10 inches will accommodate almost every book of this type. In addition, it is usual to provide one or two racks with sloping shelves, having a beading on the fore-edge of each, for the display of the large picture books used by very small children.

On the buttresses, if there are any, should be placed framed screens to take illustrations, notices, reading lists, and other suitable matter. Soft deal, covered with green baize and framed in oak, makes as good a screen as any. There should, of course, be a picture rail running round the walls, and all of the wall space not occupied by the lantern screen should be devoted to suitable pictures. These should be chosen as carefully as the books. They should be large, of recognized artistic merit, and, if possible, make some appeal to children. I do not mean by this that they should be pictures of children or definitely for children, but such pictures as Watts's *Sir Galahad*, and the *Madonna della Sedia* of

THE EQUIPMENT OF THE LIBRARY

Raphael are two among many that will occur to art lovers as possible pictures. Sometimes statuary is introduced, but it must be small and very good; good casts of *The Winged Victory* are, perhaps, typical.

4

The movable furniture consists of tables, writing tables, chairs, and a desk for the librarian. Tables and chairs are best if they are of a size suitable for children. Two heights have been found to be satisfactory for tables; 23 inches for small children and 27 inches for older ones. The seats of chairs to correspond with these tables should be 14 inches and 16 inches respectively; little children, of course, find it uncomfortable to read with their feet dangling above the floor, and too high a table is equally uncomfortable. It is well to divide the room so that the little ones have their own separate part of it. Tables may be round, rectangular, or oval. I prefer that the monotony of the room should be broken by varying them, but this is not always possible. In appearance, and in separating the readers, the round table is best, but children who are writing prefer square or oblong shapes. Tables used for writing should be covered with some substance to protect the wood from inkstains. I have found a dark blue cork carpet which is framed on to the table tops quite satisfactory.

Where the library serves at times as a lecture room it is advisable to use tables which fold up.

The tables in the Croydon Central Children's Library, described on page 107, are folding tables of this type. They were manufactured by Libraco. Writing tables imply ink stands; these should be of a very heavy type that cannot be overturned by ordinary shaking of the table, or other common accidents.

Ordinary windsor chairs are suitable, but if armchairs can be provided such as those in the Leeds libraries they are better. These are shown in the illustration facing page 112, as also is an effective stand for the display of books to which it is desired to draw special attention.

5

To make our library into a lecture room, if we have one wall with a reasonably large flat surface which is so situated that a lantern can be brought to bear upon it from some convenient place in the room, this can be painted a dead white, or, better still, with a silvery paint, to serve as a permanent lantern screen. It is essential that this should be kept quite clean and intact, and it is a good plan to have a curtain over the screen to protect it when not in use. A lantern and accessories are a part of our equipment. The choice of this depends upon the shape and size of the room, and the kind of illuminating power available. This knowledge is best obtained locally.

For lectures the part of the room below the

THE EQUIPMENT OF THE LIBRARY

screen should be raised to form a platform. The platform equipment is a movable reading desk with a light on it, and pointer and blackboard; and a method of signalling to the lecturer—an electric wire communication between the lanternist's stand and the lecturer's desk, with an electric bell-push for the lecturer, is the simplest and best. The platform should be covered with a good linoleum in order to deaden sound; lecturers move about considerably when lecturing.

6

Children are admitted to every part of the room of a modern library. Sometimes their entrance and exit are controlled by wickets of the type usually used in open access lending libraries. These wickets are, however, not essential. There should be at the entrance to the room a table so arranged that the children form themselves into queues in passing it on one side going in and on the other side going out. This table or counter should be equipped with drawers, a surface for holding the charging system, and cash till, and space for receiving returned books. Usually, in addition, the children's librarian has a proper writing desk, with drawers to hold card files, vertical files, stationery and other material essential for her work. Of course, suitable chairs are necessary accompaniments to these.

A definite space in the room must be given to a table or stand to hold the card or other catalogue.

The Norbury Children's Library, Croydon

This should be conspicuous to every child who enters the room and readily to the hand of the librarian. The counter or charging desk should have telephone equipment or at least connexion by house telephone with other departments of the library.

7

The treatment of floors in children's libraries differs. A good maple block floor kept well oiled is satisfactory; some librarians prefer rubber tiling, and where this has been used it has given eminently satisfactory results and reduces noise more effectively than any other covering. Cork carpet of a good thickness is one of the most satisfactory coverings. Sometimes coloured carpets are used here and there in the room, but these are not entirely unobjectionable as they harbour dust.

8

Some libraries provide lavatory accommodation for the children. It is no doubt a very great convenience to have a place where the child can wash, as he frequently wishes to come into the library straight from playing in the streets, and the average healthy boy is naturally dirty superficially. If it is provided, however, the staff must exercise severe supervision over it.

THE EQUIPMENT OF THE LIBRARY

9

It will not be superfluous perhaps to mention that a large number of small supplies are required. Stationery will include writing paper, scrap paper and blotters, pens and ink, erasers, rulers, a tee square, a reading glass and various other items. There will be, in addition, the whole equipment of the charging system.

10

The charging of books to borrowers is usually done on what is described as the book-card plus readers' card system. That is to say every reader has a card on which his name and address and the date of the card's validity appear. Every book has appropriated to it a card with its accession number, class-mark and the name of its author and its title. While the book stands on the shelf the book-card is kept in a pocket which is pasted on the front board under the board-label (see page 77). When the book is charged to a reader, this book-card is withdrawn from the book and "married" with the reader's card in a separate pocket; as shown on page 122.

Sometimes, instead of a loose pocket, a reader's card in the form of a pocket is used, as shown in illustration, page 123.

The date-label (see page 78), is stamped with the date the book is due to be returned. The charges, when made, are arranged numerically (or sometimes by the class-mark, or even by the names of readers) in trays behind a guide which bears the date of

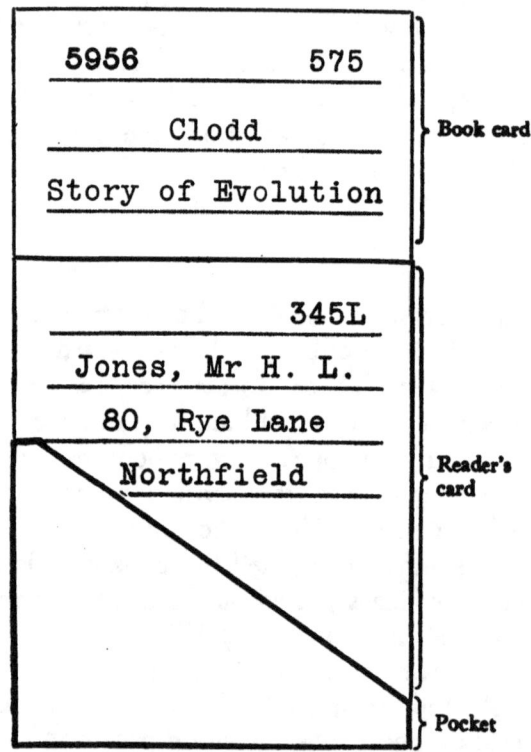

return. Charging systems are standardized library furniture which can be obtained from several of the firms specializing in library appliances.

THE EQUIPMENT OF THE LIBRARY

II

Our pictures show typical children's libraries in which the furniture may be studied. A very beautiful example is that of the Hunslet Branch Junior Library at Leeds, which was opened recently. In its treatment of the windows, its low shelves with

```
No._____

_____

_____

Expires_____
```

Northfield Public Libraries

JUNIOR LENDING LIBRARY

Take care of this Card.

It must not be lent to another boy or girl, because you are responsible for all books borrowed upon it.

If you change your address, tell the Librarian.

PLEASE DO NOT FOLD THIS CARD

appropriate facias lettered to interest and guide, the vases on the bookcases, the alternating round and square pedestal tables, the capital arm-chairs, the attractive display slopes for special books and prints, and the attractive fireplace at the end, it provides most of the features of the ideal children's library.

A MANUAL OF CHILDREN'S LIBRARIES

Our other illustrations show how the furniture is modified and varied, there being more pictures here or there and perhaps less ornamentation. Taste will vary in these matters, but the whole ideal is to have a room which is really beautiful, and to which the child will come again and again with affection.

AUTHORITIES

BRISCOE, W. A. Library Planning. 1927. Grafton.
BROWN, J. D. Manual of Library Economy. Chap. XXXII. 1930. Grafton.
EASTMAN, LINDA. Furniture, Fixtures and Equipment. 1927. Chicago: American Library Association.
HIRSHBERG, HERBERT S. Elements of Library Planning. 1930. Chicago: American Library Association.
REES, GWENDOLEN. Libraries for Children. Grafton.

CHAPTER IX

THE ARRANGEMENT OF BOOKS

I

The books in a library must be arranged, or as the librarian puts it, must be classified. It is clear that if we place the books on the shelves just as they are received we produce a muddle of volumes which is about as near a chaos as can be. The methods by which books are arranged have exercised librarians since libraries were merely collections of inscribed clay tablets: even the librarians of Pergamos divided their tablets into those which dealt with the Heavens and those which dealt with the Earth. To-day it is still best to follow in more modern style the method thus indicated, and to arrange our books by the subjects of which they treat. In larger libraries, where the children's library is a department of a system of libraries, the aim has usually been to supply in the child's library a simplified version of the classification in use in the adult departments, so that familiarity with its use may be the introduction to them. The professional children's librarian will, therefore, be familiar with the four schemes of classification, devised by librarians, which have most acceptance in public libraries—the Decimal System, the Subject System, the Library of Congress and the Classification Décimale of the Institut International de Bibliographie. But I hope there will be amongst my readers those who are not thus equipped, for whom a few simple directions will not be without value.

2

The most widely used classification is the Decimal Classification, which was invented by an American librarian, Melvil Dewey, in 1876, and has been extended and modernized continuously since. It divides the field of knowledge into ten parts as follows:—

- 0   General Works.
- 1   Philosophy.
- 2   Religion.
- 3   Sociology.
- 4   Language.
- 5   Science.
- 6   Useful Arts.
- 7   Fine Arts
- 8   Literature.
- 9   History, Biography, Geography and Travel.

Each of these *main classes*, as they are called, divides into ten *divisions*; for example,

- 50   Science, General.
- 51   Mathematics.
- 52   Astronomy.
- 53   Physics.
- 54   Chemistry.
- 55   Geology.
- 56   Palæontology.

THE ARRANGEMENT OF BOOKS

57 Biology.
58 Botany.
59 Zoology.

And each of these again into ten *sub-divisions*; i.e.,

530 Physics, General.
531 Mechanics.
532 Liquids. Hydraulics.
533 Gases. Pneumatics.
534 Sound. Acoustics.
535 Light. Optics.
536 Heat.
537 Electricity.
538 Magnetism.
539 Molecular Physics.

A further series of ten digits divides these into *sections*, as the following shows:—

537   Electricity, General.
537·1   Theory. Nature.
537·2   Static.
537·3   [Blank for future subjects.]
537·4   Atmospheric. Lightning rods.
537·5   Dynamic.
537·6   Electro-dynamics.
537·7   Electric measurements.
537·8   Appreciations.
537·9   Tables. Problems. Questions.

and the process can be continued indefinitely. The decimal character of the scheme is clearly seen, a new set of ten digits being introduced whenever a new subject appears.

A MANUAL OF CHILDREN'S LIBRARIES

3

The children's librarian may be alarmed at the apparent elaboration and minuteness of this system; but in practice it does not present any difficulty. The child is not expected to learn these figures, but merely to remember that all books on Botany, for example, bear some part of the number 580 and are arranged in that order on the shelves. Few, if any, adult users of libraries ever fathom the mysteries of the notation; all they know is that books on a subject are kept together and bear the same number. In a rather long experience I have found that there is really no need for a simpler form of classification for children's books than is used for adult books, but, as I have said, it is usual to simplify, or at least to select, from the larger classification; and certainly no children's library actually uses a tenth part of such a scheme as the Dewey classification. Moreover, I want this book to be as self-contained as possible, so that any person placed in charge of a children's library who is otherwise inexperienced may be able to work it sensibly without other aid. The following is a "selection" abridgment of Dewey, which will be found to meet all ordinary requirements. I have retained a three-figure basis throughout, as this makes the numbers —the notation—symmetrical.

THE ARRANGEMENT OF BOOKS

000 General Works
[which are too miscellaneous to go elsewhere; there are very few at this number as a rule].
010   Bibliographies, Catalogues, Lists of Books.
[When these lists deal with a particular subject, they are usually placed with that subject; i.e. a list of books on birds would go at 598·2; but some prefer to keep all lists together here.]
020   Children's Libraries.
030   Encyclopædias.
040   Essays.
050   Magazines.
060   Societies.
070   Newspapers.

100 Philosophy: General.
150   The Mind.
160   Logic.
170   Ethics: Conduct.
172   Duties of Citizenship.
173   Duties of Parents and of Children.
177   Courtesy.
178   Temperance.
179   Cruelty [to Animals, etc.].
180   Stories and Works about Ancient Philosophers.
190   Stories and Works about Modern Philosophers.

200 Religion: General.
220   Bible as a whole.
221   Old Testament.
225   New Testament.
230   The Christian Religion.
250   Church Guides, Classes, etc.
260   The Prayer Books, Hymns.
[Not hymns with tunes, which go in Music at 783.]
266   Missions.
268   Sunday Schools.

270	History of the Christian Church.
272	Persecutions. Martyrs.
274	The Christian Church in England.
280	Sections of the Christian Church: The Early Church.
282	Roman Catholic Church.
283	Church of England.
284	Other Christian Churches.
290	Non-Christian Religions.
292	Myths: Greek and Roman.
293	Myths: Teutonic and other European.
296	Jewish Church.
297	Mohammedanism.

300	**Social Sciences.**
312	Population.
320	Form of State.
324	The Vote. Elections.
325	Colonies. Emigration and Immigration.
326	Slavery. Emancipation.
327	Relations with Foreign Countries.
328	Parliaments.
330	Political Economy.
331	Workers and Employers.
332	Money and Banks.
333	Land.
335	Socialism.
336	Taxes and Rates.
337	Customs Duties (taxes).
339	Poverty.
340	Law.
350	Government.
352	Local or Town Government.
353	United States Government.
355	Military Science.
359	Naval Science.

360	Welfare Institutions and Societies.
362	Hospitals. Asylums, Orphanages.
365	Prisons.
368	Insurance.
369	Boy Scouts.
369.4	Girl Guides. Campfire Girls, etc.
370	Schools.
371	Teachers, their Training and Methods.
372	Elementary Schools (Private and Council).
373	Secondary, and Public Schools (like Eton, Rugby, etc.).
378	College and University.
380	Commerce and Communication.
383	Post Office. Stamps.
389	Weights and Measures.
390	Customs.
395	Etiquette.
396	Women.
397	Gipsies.
398	Folk-lore. Proverbs.
400	**Language.**
420	English Language.
421	Spelling.
422	Forms of Words.
423	Dictionaries.
425	Grammar.
426	Prosody.
430	German. ⎫
440	French. ⎬
450	Italian. ⎬ Divided like 420.
460	Spanish. ⎬
470	Latin. ⎬
480	Greek. ⎬
490	Other Languages. ⎭

A MANUAL OF CHILDREN'S LIBRARIES

500 Science.
510   Mathematics.
511   Arithmetic.
512   Algebra.
513   Geometry.
520   Astronomy.
530   Physics. Mechanics. Liquids. Gases.
534   Sound.
535   Light.
536   Heat.
537   Electricity and Magnetism.
540   Chemistry.
548   Crystals.
549   Minerals.
550   Geology.
560   Fossils.
570   Biology. Archæology.
572   Man and his History.
575   Evolution.
576   Life: its Origin and Properties.
578   Microscopy.
579   Collecting and Preserving Specimens.
580   Botany.
582   Flowers.
585   Trees.
589   Mosses.
590   Animals.
593   Insects. Butterflies.
594   Molluscs.
597   Fishes.
598   Reptiles.
598.2   Birds.
599   Mammals.

THE ARRANGEMENT OF BOOKS

600	**Useful Arts.**	
610		Health.
620		Engineering.
621		Mechanical Engineering.
621.1		Steam Engineering. Locomotives.
621.3		Electrical Engineering.
621.4		Air and Gas Engineering.
621.7		Factories.
622		Mining.
623		Naval and Military Engineering.
625		Railway and Road Engineering.
629		Aerial Engineering.
629.1		Aircraft lighter than air.
629.2		Aircraft heavier than air.
629.3		Motor cars. Automobiles.
630		Farming.
635		Gardening.
636		Domestic Animals and Birds.
637		Dairies.
638		Bees.
639		Hunting and Fishing (for food).
640		Domestic Economy.
641		Food.
642		Serving the Table.
643		The Home.
644		Heating, Lighting, etc.
645		Furniture.
646		Clothing. Sewing. Knitting.
648		Laundry.
649		Care of Children.
650		Communication. Business.
652		Typewriters. Cyphers. Codes.
653		Shorthand.
654		Telegraph. Cables. Signals.
655		Printing and Publishing.
656		Railroading. Sea-transport, etc.

657	Accounts, Book-keeping.
658	Business methods.
659	Advertising.
660	Chemical Manufactures.
662	Explosives. Fireworks. Fuels.
663	Beverages. Beer. Wine. Spirits. Mineral waters.
664	Foods.
665	Oils and Gases.
666	Glass. China. Porcelain.
667	Dyeing.
668	Soap. Glycerine. Glue, etc.
669	Metals.
670	Manufactures of articles made of metal, or wood, leather, fur, paper, etc.
677	Articles made of Flax, Cotton, Silk, and Metal Fibres.
678	— Rubber.
679	— Celluloid.
680	Mechanic Trades.
681	Watch and Clock making. Spectacles. Field Glasses and similar fine mechanism.
682	Blacksmithing.
684	Carriage making.
686	Bookbinding.
689	Other Trades.
690	Building Trades.
694	Carpentry.

700	**Fine Arts.**
720	Architecture.
730	Sculpture.
740	Drawing. Design.
750	Painting.
760	Engraving.
770	Photography.
780	Music.

THE ARRANGEMENT OF BOOKS

790	Recreations.
792	Theatre and Cinema.
793	Parties.
794	Indoor Games.
795	Card Games.
796	Outdoor Sports.
796·3	Football.
796·35	Cricket.
797	Boating. Swimming.
798	Horsemanship.
799	Angling. Hunting.
820	Literature written in English. (Its History, Criticism, etc.).
821	Poetry.
822	Drama.
823	About Fiction. [Not Fiction itself, which is F. (See the end of the classification.)]
824	Essays.
825	Humour.
828	Anthologies.
830	Literature in German.
840	— French.
850	— Italian.
860	— Spanish.
870	— Latin.
880	— Greek.

All divided like 820.

900	**History of the World** as a whole.
910	**Geography of the World** as a whole.
912	Atlases. Maps. Plans.
914	Geography of Europe.
915	— Asia.
916	— Africa.
917	— America.

918   Geography of South America.
919   —   Australia.

[These numbers are divided like 940–999. Thus, the history of England is 942; i.e. 9 = History, 4 = Europe and 2 = England. Travel in England is 914.2; i.e. 91 = Travel, 4 = Europe and 2 = England. 973 is the History and 917.3 the Geography of the United States, and so throughout.]

920   **Biography:** Collections of Lives.
921   Biography: Individual Lives.

[Arrange lives alphabetically in order of the names of the persons whose lives are told.]

930   **Ancient History** to A.D. 476.
931   China.
932   Egypt.
933   Judea.
934   India.
935   Medo-Persia.
936   Germans. Celts. Slavs.
937   Rome. Italy.
938   Greece.
939   Other countries.

        Modern History from A.D. 476.
940   Europe.
941   Scotland.
941·5   Ireland.
942   England and Wales.
943   Germany.
944   France.
945   Italy.
946   Spain. Portugal.
947   Russia.

THE ARRANGEMENT OF BOOKS

948	Scandinavia. Denmark.
949	Other European Countries.
950	Asia.
951	China.
952	Japan.
953	Arabia.
954	India.
955	Persia.
956	Turkey in Asia.
	Mesopotamia. Palestine. Syria, etc.
957	Siberia.
958	Afghanistan. Turkistan. Baluchistan.
959	Farther India.
960	Africa.
961	North Africa.
962	Egypt.
963	Abyssinia.
964	Morocco.
965	Algeria.
966	North Central Africa.
967	South Central Africa.
968	South Africa.
969	Madagascar and Islands of the S. Indian Ocean
970	North America.
971	Canada. Newfoundland. Labrador.
972	Mexico. Central America.
973	United States.
980	South America.
990	Oceana.
991	Malaysia.
992	Sunda. Sumatra. Java.
993	Australasia. New Zealand.
994	Australia.
995	New Guinea.
996	Polynesia.
997	Isolated Islands.

998   Arctic Regions.
999   Antarctic Regions.

Fiction forms so large a part of the library that it is best to take it from its right place at 823, give it a special class-mark, and arrange it alphabetically by the name of authors. F is the symbol usually chosen, and sometimes this is sub-divided to show special kind of stories; i.e.,

> F   Tales and Stories.
> FA   Animal and Bird Stories.
> FD   Detective Stories.
> FE   Exploration Stories.
> FF   Fairy Stories.
> FH   Historical Stories.
> FM   Military Stories.
> FN   Naval Stories.
> FR   Redskin Stories.
> FS   School Stories.

and so on. The division is difficult to make satisfactorily, but is very useful at times.

It is strongly recommended that some such scheme should be followed, as this will familiarize children with the most general practice of public libraries. There are other schemes, but as the Government Report on Public Libraries, 1927, leaned to the view that all libraries should adopt Dewey or the Library of Congress Classification, and as the latter is not obviously suitable for a children's library, enough has been said in favour of this recommendation.

THE ARRANGEMENT OF BOOKS

4

The classification number should be written in the book, on the title-page or on the back of it, and is usually shown on the back of the cover. Tags are sometimes used—Dennison's A/85 is as good as any—for the back. But there are white inks that find favour with some; and recently Gaylord Bros., whose agents in England are Messrs. Sinclair and Woolston of Nottingham, have placed on sale an electric stylus, by means of which numbers can be etched on in gold, or black or white very easily. The best method, but the most expensive initially, is to have classification numbers stamped on in gold by a bookbinder. As tags and inks both wear off, the most expensive way often proves to be the cheapest in the long run.

It is usual to add on the cover some author mark by which the book may be further arranged. For example, there will be several books on Botany in the library at the number 580. It is usual to arrange them alphabetically (within the number, of course) by the names of the authors; and this is indicated sufficiently by using the first three letters of the author's name; thus:—

$\dfrac{580}{\text{HEN}}$ Henslow's Botany.

$\dfrac{580}{\text{HOO}}$ Hooker's Botany.

$\dfrac{580}{\text{SOW}}$ Sowerby's Botany.

These examples show the class-number and the author number written in the orthodox way, in the form of a fraction. The approved position for this fraction is one inch and a half from the bottom of the book.

The books are arranged on the shelves by the class-number, and then alphabetically within that number, by the names of the authors. The only exceptions from this are books which are anonymous, which are arranged by the first word not an article in the title; and, in the case of individual biographies, alphabetically by the names of the persons whose lives are told, as is shown in the foregoing tables at the number 921.

5

When the books are on the shelves some indications of their position are necessary. An index of subjects in the classification is the simplest and most obvious of these. Perhaps a few extracts from a little guide which I have found successful will afford a clue to what is possible here:—

How to Find Books: an Index to the Subjects of the Books in the Junior Library.

If you will read this carefully and use the index that follows you will learn how the books are arranged on the library shelves and be able to find anything you want immediately.

The library is "classified"; that is to say, every book is arranged by the subject with which it deals. The index is a

THE ARRANGEMENT OF BOOKS

list of the subjects; every subject has a number; that number is written or stamped on the back of the books, and by that number the books themselves are arranged on the shelves, and entries of them are also so arranged in the "subject" card catalogue.

These are the great *classes* into which the books are divided:—

    000–099 General Works, Magazines, Encyclopædias.
    100–199 Philosophy, Conduct.
    200–299 Religion, Christianity, the Bible, and Religions which are not Christian.
    300–399 Sociology, Government, the Army and Navy, Schools.
    400–499 Languages, English and Foreign.
    500–599 Science, Mathematical, Physical and Natural.
    600–699 Useful Arts, Trades, Manufactures.
    700–780 Fine Arts, Painting, Architecture, Music, etc.
    790–799 Recreative Arts, Indoor and Outdoor Games.
    800–899 Literature, Poetry, Drama, Essays, Letters.
    900–999 History, Travel and Biography.
    F A–Z   Stories, Fiction.

It is useful, but not necessary, for you to learn these names. All you need to do is to look in the index for the subject in which you are interested, find its number, and then look for the number in order on the shelves. The numbers are decimal numbers which you will easily understand with a little practice.

Remember:—

    1. Books in a lending library are naturally often "out." Don't make up your mind that there is no book on your subject if you cannot find it on the shelf. Look in the *subject card catalogue* under the number; *that will show you all the books on your subject in the Library.*

    2. The number is a *subject* number, not the number of

only one book. Thus, the number for Travel in India is 915·4. There are several books on Indian travel in the Library, and all are numbered 915·4 on their backs. By this means you will see that all books on Indian travel are together.

3. When you have taken a book from the shelves and do not wish to borrow it, be careful to replace it *by the number*. This helps to keep the library in order, and saves your time and that of others.

4. It will give the Librarian great pleasure to explain anything that you do not understand.

Finally : This index does not show all the subjects to be found in the books, but will give you a good idea of many of them. New books, dealing with these and other subjects, will be added continually.

SUBJECT INDEX.

Adventures, Stories	F
Adventures, Travel	910
Aeroplanes	629·2
Africa, History	960–69
Africa, Travel	916
Africa, South, Travel	916·8
Africa, West, Travel	916·6
Agriculture	630
Airships	629·1
Alfred the Great	942
[Not lives, which are 920]	
Albert N'Yanza, Travel	916·7
Algebra	512
Allegories	F
Alsace-Lorraine, History	944
America, History	970
America, South, Travel	918
America, Tropical, Travel	917·2
Anglo-Saxon History	942

THE ARRANGEMENT OF BOOKS

A short extract only of the index is given, to show the method, which is to make an alphabet of every subject and synonym for it that occurs in the classification, and to add the class-mark.

6

If the library were for children of a given age, the best way to put the books on the shelves would be in the exact order of the classification scheme; but, in general, this is not possible or desirable. Books for children separate best into groups:—

1. Picture books.
2. Books for the very young.
3. Books for children between (say) 9 and 14.
4. Books for older children.

We get, therefore, four parallel arrangements of the classification. Picture books are sometimes kept lying on their sides on special stands which display their usually brilliant colours; and in any case they cannot economically be shelved with such books as Beatrix Potter's *Story of Peter Rabbit* and other tiny books for the very young. Thus groups 1 to 2 form two separate sequences from other books. Both are frequently required by adults who want to read them to children, and their separation is a practical matter for that reason. The bulk of the library will be group 3, but even here there will sometimes be large books, over ten inches in height, which it is economical to separate from the bulk. Group 4, books for older children—the collection for adolescents—offers the librarian a chance of "carrying over" the child in his or her teens to the adult library. And, again, this separate section is a practical convenience.

7

In addition to all these there is the collection of reference books, which clearly may represent most or many of the subjects in the classification. As these books are not lent out of the library they must also be kept separate. We see thus that it is impossible to make a one sequence arrangement of the library. All these arrangements must be clearly marked by guides placed over the appropriate collections. The guides most in use are:—

| PICTURE BOOKS |

| FOR OUR YOUNGEST READERS |

| FOR OLDER BOYS AND GIRLS |

| REFERENCE BOOKS
To be read in the library
Not to be taken away |

THE ARRANGEMENT OF BOOKS

As should be the case with all guides, these notices should be artistic, and should be glazed and framed.

Over each tier of shelves a guide to the classification of the books in it may be placed. The simpler these are the better; some such guides as:—

> 000 General Books.
> 200 Religion.
> 400 Languages.

are often used. Black-and-white guides are to be avoided; colour should be introduced whenever it is possible to do so. I prefer pictorial guides, and very good ones have been made by mounting and framing picture postcards of appropriate subjects required, the directions being written on the mount:—

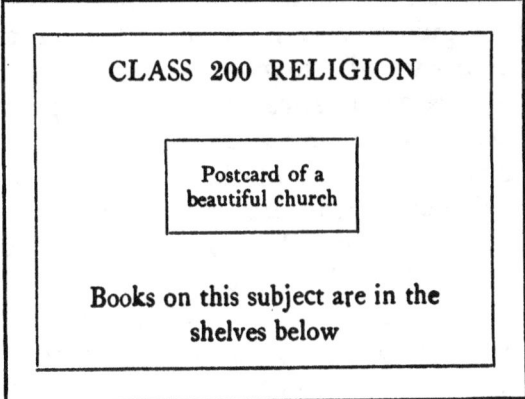

or nicely engrossed quotations can form a feature of such a guide, in this way:—

---

923 LIVES OF FAMOUS PEOPLE

> 𝔏ives of great men all remind us
> 𝔚e can make our lives sublime,
> 𝔄nd, departing, leave behind us
> 𝔉ootprints on the sands of time.

Books of Lives are in the shelves below

The idea can be developed just as far as the librarian thinks is appropriate. Do not overdo guides or notices. An isolated guide has what the advertising expert calls an "attention value," which is lost in a crowd of guides, and it is the attention of the children that we wish to gain.

In very large libraries there will be guides to individual subjects fastened on the edges of shelves; and dummies which are blocks of wood bearing the author, title and class-mark of books which do not go into the ordinary or bulk section are inserted in that section where these books would be had they been of the right size or sort, directing the reader to where they are to be found. These and other elaborations will be found described in the works on classification by the present writer listed below.

THE ARRANGEMENT OF BOOKS

They are not likely to be required in the library with less than 5,000 volumes.

8

I am conscious that I have described only one of the four schemes of classification which have general acceptance amongst librarians; but in general all library classifications follow the same laws of order and division. A trained librarian could adopt any one of them for a children's library. What I have aimed at here is to give an outline which anyone who has no access to the schemes in general can use with the assurance that it is in accordance with the method most usual in British and American public libraries.

AUTHORITIES

MANN, MARGARET. Introduction to Cataloguing and the Classification of Books. 1930. Chicago: American Library Association.

SAYERS, W. C. BERWICK. An Introduction to Library Classification. 1930. Grafton.

—— A Manual of Classification for Librarians and Bibliographers, 1926. Grafton.

CHAPTER X

THE CATALOGUE AND HOW TO MAKE IT

1

The library must be catalogued. There is no part of the librarian's task which seems simpler but is really more difficult than the making of the list of books which is called a catalogue. The conditions already laid down for classification apply for cataloguing: where the library is a department of a larger library it should follow the same catalogue forms that are in use throughout; the only difference being that the terms should be made as simple as possible. What follows, then, is a simple account of how to catalogue a library for those who have not passed through a course of cataloguing study.

2

The basis of all catalogues is the author entry, as it is called. An analysis of a rather full title-page will give us what we want to know about it.

The librarian divides this into:—

1. *The Author* = Gibson, J.

    If the forename were known it would be written in full. If it were a compound name, as Jones-Gibson,

CAMPING OUT FOR ALL

A COMPLETE HANDBOOK FOR ALL WHO LOVE THE OUT-OF-DOORS

BY

J. GIBSON

Amateur Camping Club

AUTHOR OF

"*Camp Cookery,*" "*Business Man's Diary,*" *etc., etc.*

GALE & POLDEN, LTD.
2, Amen Corner, Paternoster Row, London, E.C.4
Aldershot and Portsmouth

Copyright under Act of 1911

PRICE . . . TWO SHILLINGS NET

it would be written that way, i.e. under the first part of the compound. If the book were anonymous it would be entered under the first word not an article of the title, i.e. under "Camping."

2. *The Title* = Camping out.

A capital is used for the first word only in most catalogues, an ugly convention we have adopted to save a run on capital letters.

3. *The Sub-Title* =: a complete handbook for all who love the out-of-doors.

The sub-title is introduced by a colon (:) as shown. Sub-titles are omitted as a rule when they add nothing informative to the title. Our example has very little value, but it does show that a comprehensive character is claimed for the book.

4. *Collation* = Date. Illustrations. Portraits. Maps (if any). No. of volumes (or pages if under 100).

This information must sometimes be sought for by an examination of the book. The title-page we are considering does not show that the book is illustrated, but this is necessary information. Write the collation in this form:—

1911. Illustrated. Portraits. Maps. 81 pages.
It is well to avoid abbreviations in this catalogue, but if they are necessary the recognized ones are:—
Illus. Ports. Mps. pp.

5. *Imprint* = Gale & Polden.

And the particulars about the author suggest a note explaining his qualifications for writing his book, and so we get

6. *Annotation* = (A brief non-critical description of the author and such features of the book as are not revealed by the title-page).

THE CATALOGUE AND HOW TO MAKE IT

The resultant entry for our book in an author catalogue is therefore:—

GIBSON, J. Camping out: a complete handbook for all who love the out-of-doors. 1911. Illustrated. 81 pages. Gale & Polden.

    The author, who is a member of the Amateur Camping Club, has endeavoured "to make this book the combined experience and ideas" of many practical everyday campers. Everything in it "has been tried and found of proven worth."

Nearly everything required in the catalogue of a children's library is given in this entry, but a few further points are to be noted.

1. When a book has two authors, write them this way:—

   STEVENSON, ROBERT LOUIS, and OSBORNE, LLOYD. The ebb-tide.

   When more than two, place it under the first with *and Others*:—

   BROOKS, ERNEST, *and Others*. Out-door games.

2. When a book is anonymous, place it under the first word not an article of the title.

3. When it is pseudonymous (i.e. the author writes under a pen-name) place the book under that unless he has become better known later under his real name; i.e.—

   DONOVAN, DICK (Not J. E. MUDDOCK).
   ELIOT, GEORGE (Not MARIAN EVANS).

4. School publications, magazines, etc., go under the name of the school, i.e.—

   CHARTERHOUSE SCHOOL. The Carthusian.

   All other periodicals are best placed under their names.

A Sheaf Catalogue
Courtesy of Libraco Ltd.

A Sheaf Catalogue Open to Show Method of Consultation
Courtesy of Libraco Ltd.

5. An anthology or collection goes under its Editor, thus:—

> RHYS, ERNEST (Editor). The old country; a book of love and praise of England.

Some of the books above require what are called cross-references; that is to say, entries from that part of a joint name which is not the entry word, from the real name or pseudonym, as the case may be, to the name chosen; from the second of two authors in a joint authorship. The cataloguer makes these thus:—

> GIBSON, G. JONES-, *See* JONES-GIBSON, J.
> OSBORNE, LLOYD, *See* STEVENSON, R. L.
> MUDDOCK, J. E., *See* DONOVAN, DICK.
> EVANS, MARIAN, *See* ELIOT, GEORGE.

3

The entries are usually made on slips of paper, about 6 by 2 inches in size, one slip being used for each entry. In making these accuracy is the cheapest as well as otherwise the most satisfactory policy. When written and corrected the entries can be used in making any form of catalogue. If it is desired to print the catalogue, the printer will set up his type from them; and even if a manuscript form, such as the sheaf, or the card form, is adopted, it will still be the best plan to make the first entry on slips.

4

Taking the author slip as we have produced it above, we have to decide next in what form it shall

THE CATALOGUE AND HOW TO MAKE IT

reach the children or other users of the library. There are three well-known forms of catalogue, called 1, the Author; 2, the Dictionary; and 3, the Classified catalogues respectively.

The *author catalogue* consists of the author entries arranged in alphabetical order. It is very simple to make, and requires in addition to the author entries only the cross-references we have shown to be necessary for compound-names, joint-authors and pseudonyms. The catalogue is limited in its value as it gives information only to those who know what authors to look for; it tells nothing of what books are about.

The *dictionary catalogue* arranges in one alphabet, like the words in a dictionary, entries of a authors, b titles, c subjects, d series. Thus a book called

The Great Navigator: a life of James Cook. By Harold Peters. Famous Sailors Series.

would receive entries as follows:—

Principal entry. Peters, Harold. The great navigator: a life of James Cook. Famous Sailors Series.

Subject entry. Cook, James. Peters, Harold. The great navigator.

Title entry. The great navigator: a life of James Cook. By Harold Peters.

Series entry. Famous Sailors.
Cook, James. By Harold Peters.
Nelson, Horatio, Viscount. By Clowes James, etc.

The entries in this kind of catalogue are made under the specific subject of the book. Thus Dean Hole's

Book of the Roses, goes under Roses, not under Botany or Gardening, the larger classes to which rose-growing belongs. Under such broad heads go only such books as

Gardening.
  Wright, Thomas. The garden month by month.

with other similar *comprehensive* works; and after them a reference is made to other allied and smaller subjects, i.e.

See also Botany, Roses, Sweet Peas, Tulips, etc.

The main difficulty that the compiler encounters is "under what heading shall I put a book?" An excellent aid is available in Minnie E. Sears's *List of Subject Headings for Small Libraries*, published by the H. W. Wilson Company of New York, second edition, 1926. If a good index to our classification is made on the lines of the sample given in the previous chapter, that will serve as a list of headings.

In the *classified catalogue* the entries are arranged in the order of the classification, the principle of bringing all books on a subject together and then all subjects in relation to one another. A classified catalogue is a written genealogy or pedigree of knowledge as shown in books. Again it is based on author entries. Each entry is placed under the number in the classification scheme and the catalogue is thus the classification plus entries of books inserted into it. Thus, J. Gibson's *Camping out for*

THE CATALOGUE AND HOW TO MAKE IT

all is placed in its order in Outdoor Sports at Dewey's 796; thus

796 OUTDOOR SPORTS.
>Andrews, Harry. Training for the track.
>Ayers, E. T. The bowling green.
>Baker, E. A. The Highlands, with rope and rucksack.
>Betts, *Lieutenant* J. The sword, and how to use it.
>Brimmer, F. E. Motor camp-craft.
>Camp-life and campaigning for boy scouts.
>Childs, W. M. Holidays in tents.
>Folk dances of Europe.
>Gibson, J. Camping out for all.
>Graham, Stephen. The gentle art of tramping.

and so on. This series of entries would be followed by 796·3, i.e. books on football, and that by 796·35 books on cricket, and so on throughout the classification. The classified catalogue is, therefore, a list of the books in the order in which they stand on the shelves. With this difference, however, that books which deal with more than one subject can be analysed in the catalogue. A book can go on one place only on the shelves; it can go in as many places as we like in the catalogue. Thus a book dealing with Indoor and Outdoor Games, say

>Edwards, A. R. M. Parlour and lawn games.

goes on the shelves at 794, but would be entered under both 794 and 796 in the catalogue.

The classified catalogue requires for its ready use both author and subject indexes. The index to the classification scheme itself is, of course, the

155

A Card Catalogue Cabinet
Courtesy of Libraco Ltd.

best index to such a catalogue, and a short author index, such as

> Edwards. Parlour and lawn games. 794
> Gibson. Camping. 796

is essential.

5. Forms of Catalogue

When the inner form of catalogue has been settled, we have next to determine its physical shape. The printed catalogue is in itself the best form of catalogue. It is portable, in book-form, and is easily understood. It is not always economic, however; it is out of date before it is printed, and it is costly. If it cannot be afforded, and even when it can, some form of manuscript catalogue is desirable, and there are only two forms which have any general acceptance, 1, the sheaf, and 2, the card.

The *sheaf catalogue* consists of a number of sheets held in a loose-leaf binder, called the sheaf-holder. Our illustrations will demonstrate the form better than many words.

The principle is that one entry only shall be made on each leaf of the catalogue. As the leaves are independent, complete mobility is possible; new entries can be inserted and old ones withdrawn at will. The catalogue, too, has book form, though of a somewhat extended kind.

The *card catalogue* is a more widely used application of the same principle of mobility. Each entry is made on a separate card and the cards are arranged so that they stand in drawers and can be read without removal from them. Cards and card appliances are made by many library supply firms, and the standard international card is 5 inches wide by 3 inches long.

In connexion with both card and sheaf catalogues what is called the unitary system of cataloguing is the simplest method of making it. That is to say, one catalogue entry is made and on it are written all the necessary references and indications of additional entries; thus, to repeat:—

> 796 GIBSON, J.
> C
>   Camping out for all: a complete handbook for all who love the out-of-doors. 1911. Illustrated. 81 pp. Gale & Polden.

In a dictionary catalogue three copies of this card will be required, one each under Author, Title and Subject. On the top line, which has purposely been left blank, can be written the arranging word or phrase; in this case for "Camp-craft" or "Camping," and for "Camping out." The first card, as shown and without further wording, serves as author entry.

In a classified catalogue two copies will be required, under 796 and under the author. It is assumed that the subject index will be a separate brief one as already suggested.

When a book deals with a second, third or more subjects, a card is copied for each, the number of

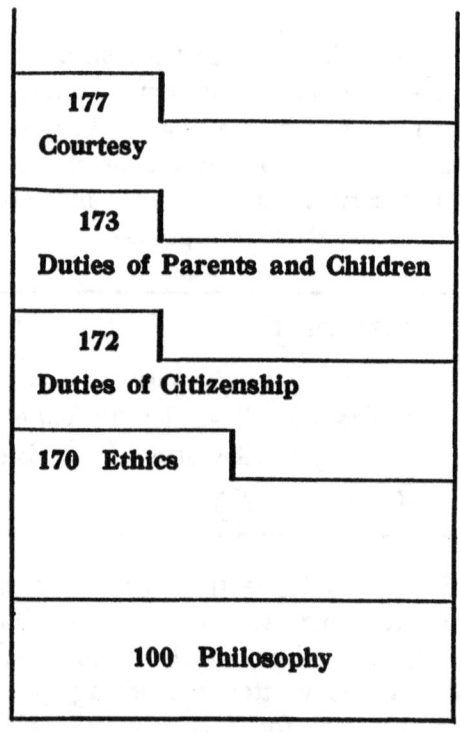

the subject being written in the left top corner in red-ink (assuming Gibson's book to have such subjects, above the 796 which is the arranging number and is always in heavy black figures). The point of the method is that one operation completes the classification and cataloguing work, the additional entries being mere copying work.

A card catalogue must be guided. On the outside of the drawers are label holders in which the numbers of the subjects catalogued on the cards within it may be shown. Inside, it is usual to use a series of guide cards which project about $\frac{1}{2}$ inch above the other cards. For main classes, General Works, Philosophy, Religion, etc., *singles* are used, for main divisions *halves*, for sub-divisions *thirds*, and so on as required. The drawer appears somewhat as on the facing page.

6. The Shelf Register

A few words may be said on the shelf register, as it is a sort of classified catalogue. It is most useful not only as a checking list, but as a rapid finding list in which books are entered more quickly than they can be as a rule in catalogues. It is a list of the books as they stand on the shelves in their class order, arranged on loose-leaves usually of quarto size, ruled horizontally, for authors and titles, and vertically to give columns for years. One sheet, or more as may be necessary, is given to every subject, the class number being written in the right-hand top corner. When it is desired to check the stock— a task which should be undertaken once a year, or, at any rate, a class at least should be checked yearly, to see what losses, if any, have been sustained—a tick is put in the column for the year for

Drawer of a Card Catalogue
Courtesy of Libraco Ltd.

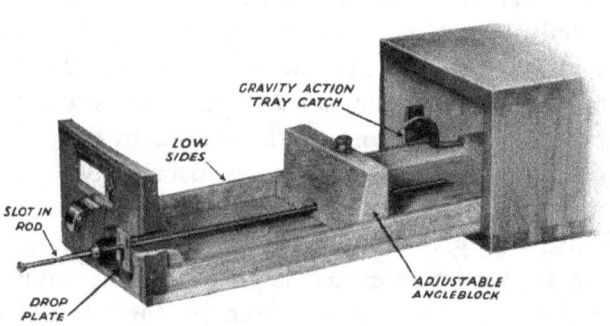

One-Drawer Card Catalogue, showing Construction
Courtesy of Libraco Ltd.

A MANUAL OF CHILDREN'S LIBRARIES

Accessions No.	Author	Title	1931	1932	1933	1934	1935	1936	1937	1938	1939	1940	1941	796
22,342	Andrews	Training for the track												
35,187	Ayers	The bowling green												
41,820	Baker	The Highlands, with rope, etc.												
44,396	Betts	The sword, and how to use it												

THE CATALOGUE AND HOW TO MAKE IT

each book as it is found to be present. The blanks direct to missing books, which can then be searched for in the many places in a library to which books travel in their careers. A ruling for such a register is given opposite, in which blank lines are left to allow insertions to be made.

AUTHORITIES

LIBRARY ASSOCIATION AND AMERICAN LIBRARY ASSOCIATION. Cataloguing Rules: author and title entries. 1930. Library Association.
[The standard of all modern cataloguing practice.]
CUTTER, C. A. Rules for a Dictionary Catalogue. Washington: Government Printing Office.
HITCHER, THERESA. Cataloguing for Small Libraries. 1915. Chicago: A.L.A.
MANN, MARGARET. Introduction to Cataloguing and the Classification of Books. 1930. Chicago: A.L.A.
QUINN, J. H. Library Cataloguing. 1913. Truslove & Hanson.
SAYERS, W. C. BERWICK, and STEWART, J. D. The Card Catalogue. 1913. Grafton.
STEWART, J. D. The Sheaf Catalogue. 1909. Libraco.

PART III
THE LIBRARIAN'S WORK

CHAPTER XI

THE LIBRARIAN AND THE WORK OF THE LIBRARY

Our library is now duly furnished and equipped, and presumably supplied with books. How is it to be worked?

1. THE CHILDREN'S LIBRARIAN

The whole success or otherwise of a library for children depends ultimately upon the staff who administer it. The choice of a librarian and the qualifications required demand careful attention—what sort of personality and what training?

There is no reason why a man should not be a children's librarian; some men have a genius for the handling of children; but experience tells me that they are not to be found in the average library personnel. Nor, I suppose, have men in general the ambition to fill this role, admirable as it undoubtedly is; and even were a man by temper and character ever so well adapted for the work, we have to assume on the whole that this particular branch of work belongs to women. What sort of woman then is required? She must like children, of course; but a mere liking for children is providentially the possession of all normal women; and that qualification in itself will not carry us far. Beyond liking there must be interest, almost an inspired interest, in their doings, aspirations, and general outlook. A children's library, however, is neither nursery nor crèche; nor is it a substitute on a rainy day for the playground. The librarian must be able to manage children, to attract them, and yet to command the most complete discipline. In fact, discipline is perhaps the main problem of the library. Good work can never be done with a mere mob of children, and nothing whatever can be done with a mob which is out of control. So we may assume that a children's librarian must be a person of good education, solid nerves, and attractive to youngsters. It is one of the most delightful but quite one of the most difficult branches of library service. She must have library training, and she must specialize in all that concerns children in school, in literature, in recreation. If we could command such training, a course in the Froebel or Montessori systems would be an ideal foundation upon which to build her library technique, but there are thus two forms of training involved, and we have not yet reached the position when it is always economically possible to demand these. Some sort of substitute is possible. Girls who have done social work—at settlements, play-centres, in the guides—and those who have taught in Sunday school, have gained an experience which has practical advantage afterwards in library life.

The hours to be worked are awkward in the extreme. Remember that libraries in general are open (and must necessarily be open) at hours when other folk are at leisure. As with the adult, so with the child; he is free for about two hours at noon—so there goes the librarian's chance of the conventional lunch hours; he is free again from 4 p.m. until bedtime—say 7 or 7.30; so there go a reasonable tea and evening dinner hour. Orthodox hours are indeed possible during school holidays; but, for the elementary school child, these amount to only two months in the twelve. When people tell me, as some of them do, I am sure conscientiously, that they would like to work in a children's library—I would have them think out all the implications of these hours. They are not long hours; they are abominably awkward ones. The children's staff should work shorter hours than other library staff, as the strain of the work is greater in almost every way.

A successful children's librarian has had some social experience, is a friend of the teachers, and visits their schools at least once a term, sometimes to talk to the children there. She must be able to organize talks, demonstrations about books, catalogues and classification for her young clients, exhibitions and story hours; indeed, she must be able to lecture and to take the story hour herself if need be.

And what are we able to pay this very perfect librarian? The answer is a little depressing, but it need not always be so. I suppose the average pay for a children's librarian is under £200 a year; or about as much as a good stenographer with a secondary school education should command. The best-paid children's librarians known to me receive salaries of between £250 and £300 yearly. I have a substantial hope that the time will come, with the general appreciation in the work of librarians, when this work will be appreciated as it ought to be; but it is useless to paint a more roseate picture now.

We have in England no schools for children's librarians; they have good ones in America, and even issue a *Year-Book of Children's Libraries*.[1] That for this year, which I have just examined, shows how wide-spread and deep is the call of this work over there, and what great care is given to its study by librarians. The schools pay special attention to child psychology, children's books, practical story-telling, and so on. In England our librarians are trained in their libraries, and there is no systematic study of the work on national lines, except the brief course of lectures at the University of London School of Librarianship.

To conclude this staff question. Assistants have to be provided in some cases. I have had one or two good ones from the School of Librarianship; but, frankly, only one person in ten is adapted physically, temperamentally and "by nature" (if one may say so) for this work; and I would advise no one to focus upon it until she is convinced of a vocation for it.

[1] American Library Association (Chicago).

LIBRARIAN AND WORK OF THE LIBRARY

2. The Librarian's Work

The library is ready, and we have our librarian. How will her day be spent? There are the hours between nine and twelve, before the children arrive. There is the careful arranging of the department, the checking of the shelves for misplaced books, and of the periodicals to see that these are all available and intact. There is the occasional setting-out of bulletin boards. These consist of the baize screens on our walls on which are illustrations of "Memories of the Month," Anniversaries, Current Events, and similar topical matters, accompanied by brief lists of books which bear upon them. The illustrations come from the Illustrations Collection, which is made up of pictures cut from withdrawn books, periodicals no longer current, trade catalogues, and numberless other sources, and are mounted on uniform-size mounts of vandyke brown or sage green nature paper. On Saturday mornings you would see a group of children cutting out and mounting these illustrations, which have been chosen by the librarian; this they do as a pastime.

While her assistant is thus engaged (if she has one), the children's librarian is engaged in checking reviews and catalogues of new books, and receiving and examining those she has ordered on approval. She may visit a school; or receive a class in school hours to whom she gives a lesson in the use of the library. She may be arranging lectures or story hours and will call upon possible lecturers or story-tellers. In my own case I prefer the children's librarian to ask personally for all the help wanted rather than to write asking for it. This is quicker, more intimate, better in results. She is expected to attend any lecture, conference, or committee in the town which seems in any way to touch her work. She has to check new applications for membership, interview callers, and deal with correspondence, and she must keep complete records of her issues, additions, and new readers. The hours when the library is "closed" are not exactly idle ones, it will be agreed.

At noon the doors are opened. At first the children come in ones or two; but by half-past twelve every seat may be occupied with readers, while others are at the shelves choosing the book to take home. Many children use the noon hour for getting on with school homework, but more are following serials in *Chums*, *The Scout*, or whatever their favourite journal may be. It is busy; it is quiet—reasonably quiet. You may be surprised to find at the counter boys and girls calmly issuing and discharging books as if they were library assistants. They *are* library assistants—voluntary ones, who at their own request are chosen by the librarian as her helpers. I am a firm believer in the theory that children should be encouraged to regard the library as their own; and it gains immensely in interest for them if they may register books, put them away on the shelves, tidy the room, and help with the mounting of illustrations.

LIBRARIAN AND WORK OF THE LIBRARY

3. The Librarian's Work: Admission of Readers

How are children admitted? Our rules are few and flexible. There is no age limit; nor should there be unless want of space demands a limitation in the numbers using the department. We say the library is "for children of school age," which may be interpreted as, from as early as a child wants *to be read to*, until he goes exclusively to the adult department of his own volition—he is never turned away because he is too old; nor is he excluded because too young. If he applies on his own initiative he must be able to read the simplest books we have—say *Peter Rabbit* or *Mother Goose*; but his parents may borrow in his name if he is too young to read and wants to be read to. No child at school is admitted without the signature of his teacher on a form saying he will benefit by the use of the library. This is not that the teacher shall make the library a reward for good conduct in the child, but in order that the teacher may be aware of the fact that the child is a reader, and may perhaps exercise some supervision over that reading. Moreover, although this signing of a form implies no moral responsibility on the part of the teacher, he does feel that he should help us to recover overdue and lost books and to keep discipline of a sort in their use. Teachers are excellent friends of librarians; but do not expect too much of them. This signature is demanded even for the child who wants to use the room only as a reference library and does not want to borrow books. Here is the form we use:—

CROYDON PUBLIC LIBRARIES

THE JUNIOR LIBRARY

Teacher's Recommendation for Reading Room and Reference Library

I believe that..................................of this school will use the Junior Reading Room and Reference Library to his/her advantage, and recommend that he/she be enrolled as a reader.

Signed..

Head Teacher of..........................School

Date..................................

FRONT OF CHILDREN'S APPLICATION FORM

JUNIOR LIBRARY

I apply to become a Reader in the Junior Reading Room and Reference Library, and I promise:—

1. To behave in a quiet and orderly manner in and near the Library buildings.
2. To come with clean hands.
3. To take great care of the books and newspapers which I find in the room.
4. To help the Librarian in every possible way to make the Library useful and pleasant both for myself and others.

Signed..

Age..

Date..................Address..............................

BACK OF CHILDREN'S APPLICATION FORM

LIBRARIAN AND WORK OF THE LIBRARY

The child signs this *in the presence of the librarian* and then is given this ticket:—

CROYDON PUBLIC LIBRARIES

THIS TICKET ADMITS

**TO THE JUNIOR
READING ROOM**

For the remainder of the rules; here are the most important. The fewer the rules the better:—

4. Rules for the use of Junior Libraries

READING AND REFERENCE DEPARTMENTS

1. Any child of school age may be admitted to the use of the Reading and Reference Departments on the recommendation of the teacher of the school which he or she attends. The recommendation shall be made on a voucher which can be obtained without charge at the Library.

2. The children are expected to behave in a quiet and orderly manner in the Library, and the Children's Librarian shall have the power to exclude any child whose conduct prevents the proper use of the Department by others, or who is uncleanly in person or otherwise offensive to other readers. No child with unclean hands shall be allowed to enter the room. Talking and eating are not permitted.

3. Certain tables are set apart for the reading of reference books, and for writing purposes. Magazines and periodicals will not be permitted to be read at these tables.

A MANUAL OF CHILDREN'S LIBRARIES

LENDING DEPARTMENT

4. Children may borrow books for home reading on the following conditions:—

(1) Children under 12 years of age must be guaranteed by a householder and their voucher of application must be countersigned by the head teacher of the school they attend.

(2) Children over 12 will be permitted to borrow on presenting an application voucher signed by a householder.

(3) A reader's ticket is not interchangeable, and must not be used by anyone other than the child named upon it.

(4) Children who are not qualified to become borrowers by residence or school attendance in the town will be allowed to borrow on payment of 5s. per annum.

5. Children under 12 may borrow one book at a time. Children over 12 may borrow two books at a time, one only of which shall be fiction.

6. Books may be retained for reading for 15 days, including the days of issue and return. If it is desired to keep a book longer it may be brought to the Library and the issue will be renewed for a further 15 days unless the book is required by another reader. A fine of One Penny per week or part of a week will be charged upon all books kept beyond the period of issue allowed. The Children's Librarian may at her discretion suspend the ticket of a borrower in lieu of charging a fine.

7. Children must take proper care of the books, protect them in wet weather, and must not mark the pages, turn down the leaves or otherwise injure the books. Lost books must be paid for, and damage to books must be paid for at the discretion of the Librarian.

LIBRARIAN AND WORK OF THE LIBRARY

GENERAL

8. On the occasion of Library Lectures or Story Hours the work of the Lending and Reading Departments may be suspended for the time being as the circumstances require.

INFECTIOUS DISEASE

9. Books which have been exposed to infection from any infectious disease must not be returned to the Libraries, but shall be sent to the Inspector of Nuisances at the Town Hall. Children who have been in contact with infection must tell the Children's Librarian and they will be instructed as to the disposal of any books they may have in their possession.

Every child receives a little booklet giving him information suitable to his age of the activities and privileges he may share and of the simple return duties expected of him.

To return to our librarian at work.

[I am presuming here that she is on duty all day from 9 a.m. to 7.30 p.m.—hours which would soon destroy her if she worked them—just to follow out a whole day's work.]

At 2 p.m. the library closes until 4 p.m., but only to the general reader; for the time is usually occupied by a class from a school which, under the direction of their teacher, has come to read, as we describe in Chapter XII.

At four o'clock a busy half-hour begins, in which the children are choosing books to read at home. There is then a more or less slack interval for their tea-time, until 5.30 p.m. Now the real work of the day begins; the children come in in some volume from now onwards until seven o'clock. Many of them have their school work to do; they go to the reference tables, and here a great opportunity occurs for the librarian to show them how to consult books, to use indexes and so on in the tracking of answers to their questions. Many teachers set every week the general knowledge questions published in *The Teachers' World*, and if the librarian looks through them she is prepared beforehand. Librarians have to recommend books for individual readers; this should never be done unless the child is at a loss or asks for help. All the books are good presumably, so there is no real fear of a *bad* choice; but when it is felt that suggestions are necessary they should be made in such manner that the youngster thinks he is doing the choosing. Say, *you* like the book; not that *he ought* to read it. Occasionally suggest a book is a little beyond him—that is most tantalizing! Remember, again, "the only book that ultimately does good to a child is the one he chooses for himself."

Six o'clock comes. This is Story-Hour time. In a corner of the room the children are gathered in a half-circle about a Story-Teller who, as I have said, may be the librarian, or may be a teacher or some other voluntary worker. Some of the so-called Story Hours are really Readings. Some libraries have Story Hours in a room adjoining the reading room and lending library; some have what is actually a Story-Hour Room. In these there is a fireplace with an electric magicoal fire; and by this the storyteller sits with the children grouped round; some on chairs, some on a coloured mat. About twenty-five children is an ideal number; but in one library I have had to admit sixty in order not to disappoint the children. This demands the more expanded treatment given in Chapter XIV.

One night in the week is Talk night. The library ceases to issue books at five o'clock. Tables are folded up and put aside, the room is chaired, and at 6 p.m. is filled with children for a lecture, which is usually illustrated with lantern slides. This is one of the most popular activities; and children have to be admitted by ticket, so great is the demand for seats. Usually these lectures are given by voluntary lecturers, but sometimes are given by members of the staff, as we show later (Chapter XIII). Lectures are over at seven, and it is usual to allow the children to return ten minutes later. (They should go out first, however, lest you have pandemonium; and the room should be put straight and ventilated.)

There may be many other activities in our librarian's day; no two days, indeed, are quite alike. There will be meetings of the children's staff once or twice a month when experiences are compared and decisions made as to work to be done or discontinued. It is a wise thing to leave off unproductive activities and to try others; some of our efforts must be less successful than others, and this must be recognized as quickly as possible.

Then, almost every season brings its appropriate

work. Christmas seems to demand seasonable decorations in the room; and for the octave of Christmas there may be a Christmas Story Festival, when stories suitable to the time are told every day to crowded audiences—*Cinderella, Ali Ba-Ba, Alice, Peter Pan,* and Dickens's *Christmas Carol* are examples. In every library in one system the *Christmas Carol* is told every year.

Some libraries have a children's dramatic society and that demands more work than is usually imagined; some have reading circles where books are discussed; some even have a cinema installation, and wireless and gramophones are all used in the educational sense. Then, brief reading lists are issued on any subject that is in the air or that it is good to bring before the children; these require careful thought to be made effective.

I have urged that discipline is the main factor in successful work. The children's librarian is invested with wide discretionary powers, as to the number of books certain children may borrow, the infliction or remission of fines for overdue books or for damage to books, or other penalties. The severest penalty is suspension from the use of the library for a time. This is seldom necessary and should be resorted to rarely.

It will now be concluded that, when 7.30 comes and the children's librarian goes home, her day has been a strenuous one. She gives more joy to her race than most people, but it is the result only of much admirable enthusiasm and self-sacrifice on her part.

LIBRARIAN AND WORK OF THE LIBRARY

I have directed this chapter to the work of the children's libraries with which I am best acquainted. I have done so deliberately in order to show the character of a children's library as I see it, and some of the topics must be dealt with further. All libraries do not carry out all this work; many do very little of it; and the forms and rules I have included are samples only, which every librarian modifies to suit his special circumstances.

AUTHORITIES

AMERICAN LIBRARY ASSOCIATION. Children's Library Year-Book. 1929. Chicago.

CLEVELAND PUBLIC LIBRARY. Work with Children and the Means used to Reach Them. 1912.

HAZELTINE, ALICE I. (Editor). Library Work with Children: reprints of papers and addresses. Classics of American Librarianship. 1917. New York: H. W. Wilson Company.

POWER, EFFIE L. Library Service for Children. 1930. Library Curriculum Series. Chicago: A.L.A.
   This work, which unfortunately appeared too late for me to use it, is put forward by the A.L.A. as its authoritative text-book.

REES, GWENDOLEN. Libraries for Children. 1924. Grafton.

CHAPTER XII

TEACHING THE USE OF THE LIBRARY

I

Of the activities of the children's librarian none is more important than that of teaching the youngsters the right use of the library. This is done individually almost daily; directions in how to find books, how to use the contents pages, indexes, dictionaries, and maps are so ordinary a part of her duties that their great importance is not likely to be overlooked. Nevertheless there are right and wrong ways of doing these things, and while I do not claim to know the best ways, a few hints from experience may not be without their value.

As we saw when we considered the selection of books, children have a natural and not always unjust suspicion of their elders who recommend "good things" to them. For example: to tell a child that he should read *The Cloister and the Hearth* because it is a classic which he ought to know, may induce him to borrow, even to attempt to read, the book; but I find that at the back of his effort may lie the feeling that it has been imposed upon him. These books usually come back to the library quietly when some other person than the one who recommended the reading is on duty, and I believe they usually

TEACHING THE USE OF THE LIBRARY

come back unread. On the other side is the librarian who tells the child that she herself is reading a book which she finds of great interest. As an afterthought she adds, "It's probably too old for you: it's Charles Reade's *The Cloister and the Hearth.*" The normal child cannot resist this challenge, and borrows the book with a determination to master it, and believing, as he ought to believe, that he has made choice himself of the book. A right understanding of the implications of this example will make a successful children's librarian; because we all do want children to read good books, to have as their familiars the masterpieces of literature. Youth is the right time for such acquaintance, and if it is not made then it is never so completely made in later years. Of course common sense suggests that the method of tantalization, if it may so be called, is not suitable for every child, nor can it be used more than once in a while with any child; but what is clear is that the librarian can make very few direct recommendations of books with entire success. We revert to the general principle laid down by the Library Association for work in children's libraries: "the aim of the library as an educational institution is best expressed in the formula, 'Self-development in an atmosphere of freedom' ... in the library the pupil strikes out his own line, and becomes his own teacher." This is the experience of the librarian, who realizes that in order to induce children to use books they must be led to believe that they do so of their own free will. Moreover, childhood is full of "days of discovery," when the child, let loose amongst good books, comes for himself upon the things he can use and like. No intervention of the librarian, or anyone else, should prevent such individual exploration.

There are, however, limits to all things, even to the will for independence in children. They will, and do, ask advice, and the librarian must be prepared to give it from her knowledge of books and of how to handle them. This need rises when the child comes to the library for help in lessons. Such help should be forthcoming, but it should merely be help; it is not the business of the librarian, it is indeed eminently undesirable for her, to do the work for the child. How and where to find his information is to be shown him by the librarian; but the actual finding the child must do. To take a few examples. A child is asked how far it is from London to Plymouth. The librarian may well show the child the scale of the map, but the measuring must not be done for him. In the search for *Kirkonnell Lea*, the librarian may put Palgrave's *Golden Treasury* into the child's hands; but she should not find the actual lyric. She should not, where school homework is concerned, give the child direct information of any kind. There is a very large field of work in showing the sources of information; there is no time, even if it were desirable, and it is not, for doing the work which ought to be done by the child himself.

TEACHING THE USE OF THE LIBRARY

2

We can do for school classes of children what can be done, whenever it is necessary, for individual children; that is to say, give lessons in the use of books and libraries. Such lessons are a desirable part of the work of the fully-equipped children's library. Two kinds of lesson are general, and there are several forms of each.

The first is the school lesson in the library. Here a class attends in school hours, under the supervision of a teacher, and reads as he (or she) directs. The lesson must be arranged ahead, if it is to be productive. It is necessary to fix the times for these class-visits, as it is found that many schools desire to make them, and it is quite obvious that the individual school cannot have them very frequently. I have found that in a large town, once a fortnight is as often as they can be managed. The teacher chooses the subject, or subjects, and gives the librarian notice of them a few days before the class comes; and it is well if the teacher realizes that literature on most subjects is limited. I remember occasions when as many as forty children have been sent by a well-meaning teacher, "to read all about Julius Caesar." Monographs and articles on the great Roman are more plentiful than they are on most subjects, but, even so, it was impossible to meet this sudden demand in a public library; other readers were interested in Julius Caesar and had borrowed many of the books. (I overcame the difficulty—badly, I admit—by putting the children in a quiet room and getting the senior amongst them to read aloud to the rest; but that is hardly library work of the sort under discussion.) The teacher should be apprised of this difficulty and will usually choose several suitable subjects that may be read simultaneously by different sections of the class. The librarian will then gather all the books on the subjects, drawing on other libraries if they are available, and on all departments if the children's library is part of a larger public library. The illustrations, collection, atlases, individual maps and other resources of the library are placed at the disposal of the teacher. The lesson is sometimes one in which there is actual personal teaching with the use of the blackboard and the other materials mentioned; but more often it is merely directed class-reading in which notes are sometimes taken which can be checked by the teacher. It is customary, however, at every such visit to give a short time, from a quarter of an hour upwards, to individual reading: the children being allowed to choose what they will read from the shelves.

Opinions differ as to the value of such library classes. It is objected that by these means the children's library becomes merely another school classroom, and that it is not the business of the library to be such. The infrequency, too, with which any class can attend makes any very deep impression from the books read impossible, and the whole business is perfunctory. Worst of all, the teacher enters the library this way, and brings not "self-development in an atmosphere of freedom," which we thought to be essential, but "training in an atmosphere of restraint or discipline" which is alleged to be the aim of the school. All these possibilities may be admitted; but another view is that schools are far less restraining institutions than is generally supposed; that the interest of the teachers is invaluable; and that the class does bring to the library and makes accustomed to it many children who would not otherwise come there. Perhaps the risk may be taken of losing a few children who through these lessons may be led to connect the idea of "school" with libraries for the sake of the numbers who may discover the libraries through them.

3

The other form of lesson has been called a "library object lesson," perhaps not very lucidly. It is given by the librarian in the use of libraries and of books. It does not deal with how to read, although lessons on that subject may well be considered as possible work for a librarian; that is to say, on how to read systematically to get the best out of books, not, of course, how to translate words into meaning. In the library lesson, however, classes of children come to the library to learn how to make the best of it. These lessons are recognized by school inspectors as a rule and may be undertaken in school time.

A MANUAL OF CHILDREN'S LIBRARIES

A brief description of one I have given frequently may suggest how it is done.

A class, accompanied by a teacher, attends at the agreed hour. It should consist of not more than twenty-five children, and a smaller number is better. The children's librarian welcomes them to the library, and points out that it is their own and that to become a member is a simple process. The library, she continues, has several parts: the newspaper room where news and the undigested thoughts of men are to be found; the periodicals room where a more considered account of news and of current thought is to be found; the lending library where are books representing the best in past and present thought and imagination which may be drawn upon for home reading; and, finally, the reference library where in their finest forms and in their most convenient shapes the books which are the sources and fullest or, again, most concentrated purveyors of knowledge are available. All this will be done in the simplest language, the purpose being to convey to the children the idea that this great civic institution is theirs to use and that it is a connected, systematic, purposeful organization. Continuing, the class is told that at present they are not old enough to enjoy to the fullest extent the resources of the adult libraries; and will probably find the junior department more to their liking, where are books specially written for them. Here, however, are all the same departments, if on a somewhat

TEACHING THE USE OF THE LIBRARY

smaller scale—newspapers and periodicals, lending and reference books.

The class is taken into the library.

The lay-out of the room is explained; and the position of reference books, lending library books, etc., is made clear.

Then follows a discussion of the question: "how do I find a book?" The group gathers round the card author catalogue. It is described: as a list of books made on cards, one card being given to each entry. Cards are withdrawn and shown to illustrate. A child is asked to name a book—it will usually be some such work as *Robinson Crusoe*—the author is identified; a child is asked to find the card.

More difficult, perhaps, but not greatly so, is the description of classified catalogue. It is explained that here there is again a card for every entry, but that it is arranged by a number. That number represents the subject of the book. To make this effective every child is given a condensed subject index, on the lines of that described in Chapter IX, page 142; but for libraries which use the full Dewey Decimal Classification an excellent little work for this purpose is published by Libraco, entitled *How to Find a Book*. A child is asked to name a subject, to look for it in the subject index and find its number, and then to find the card in the catalogue.

This leads naturally to a description of the arrangement of the books on the shelves. The librarian shows how the classes run, and explains, as simply as possible, the meaning of the terms; thus,

000. GENERAL WORKS: Works like newspapers, encyclopædias and other books which deal with so many subjects that they cannot go under any one of them. It is best to mention books by name here, and in all the following classes. If we tell a child that an encyclopædia is a general work and illustrate it from the *Children's Encyclopædia*, we shall perhaps be understood, but we probably shall not if we merely refer to general works as books which deal with everything.

100. PHILOSOPHY: The Mind and how it works and how our conduct is governed.

200. RELIGION: Books which deal with God, the Bible, worship, the history of the Christian churches, and with the religions which are not Christian, such as Mohammedanism, Buddhism, and so on.

300. SOCIOLOGY: Books about the way men live together, in families, in towns and in countries; their schools, money, government and parliaments, laws, and their customs.

400. LANGUAGES: Grammars of English and foreign languages, with works on the writing of prose and poetry and dictionaries of these languages.

500. SCIENCE: Of two kinds, mathematical and natural. The mathematical deals with arithmetic, algebra, geometry and higher mathematics. The natural with such things as astronomy, heat, light, sound, electricity, chemistry; with the earth in geology, and with the inhabitants of the earth in biology, which means life, so that we get here early man and his history, plant life, insect, animal, fish and bird life.

600. USEFUL ARTS: This is a very mixed class which begins with medicine, which is the discovery, prevention and treatment of disease, and leads on to all the trades and crafts of men, except the fine arts; thus we have books of all forms of engineering, steam, electric, as well as aerial navigation;

TEACHING THE USE OF THE LIBRARY

books on office work, shorthand, typing and book-keeping, manufactures, farming and gardening, domestic economy and building.

700. FINE ARTS: Here are books on all the methods men and women have used to beautify their surroundings, by means of fine gardening, architecture, carving, drawing, painting, photography, and music; and the recreations, that is to say, sports and games which add pleasure and grace to life.

800. LITERATURE: This consists of books in which man has used writing in a beautiful manner to give us enjoyment or to create imaginary worlds for us. Here we have poetry, plays, essays, fine speeches, and, in addition, books of humour.

900. This is a class in three parts—HISTORY, which is the story of peoples as nations; GEOGRAPHY, which is the description of the surface of the Earth, of countries and towns, and the stories and records of travellers; BIOGRAPHY, which is the lives of great men.

Then show, by a definite example, the divisions of each class, by pointing out that 9 means History, 94 the History of Europe, 942 the History of England, 942·2 the History of the South-Eastern Counties, and 942·21 the History of Surrey. Indicate then that the books within this, the most specific number, are arranged alphabetically by the names of authors.

Then give each child a copy of the subject index. Explain its use, the meaning of synonyms, etc.; that is to say, if they want books on fishing, and do not find any reference to that topic, they should look under angling; if they want petroleum, they should look under oils, and so on.

A card should then be given to each child to test the results of the lesson, and about a quarter of an hour allowed for the finding of the books.

Have the books when found brought to a special table, and explain all errors to the children.

The lesson concludes with a few words on the methods of becoming members of the library, and, if it is desirable, vouchers and circulars of information are distributed.

> Find the books on the following list. If any book is not in, bring the book of the same number nearest to the place where the missing book should be.
>
> | *Subject* | *Author* | *Title* |
> |---|---|---|
> | Architecture | Bond | Gothic Architecture. |
> | Biography | Morley | Life of W. E. Gladstone. |
> | Health | Miles | Muscle, Brain and Diet. |

CARD FOR EXERCISE IN FINDING BOOKS

I have confined this chapter to a detailed account of the way I would teach children to use a lending library. The lesson occupies rather more than an hour, and is quite as much as can be presented at a time; and personally I would prefer a lesson about half the length, were it not that the exercise in the finding of books is looked upon by the youngsters rather as a game. There are, of course, many other lessons that might and ought to be given on guides to reading, how to use reference books, and other

TEACHING THE USE OF THE LIBRARY

topics that will occur to every active librarian. The difficulty is for teachers to spare the time during school hours in these crowded days for their classes to take them; but there is no doubt that few lessons can have such a far-reaching and permanent value to the pupils.

AUTHORITIES

Model lessons have not been published on the actual lines of those advocated here, but very useful material will be found in the books below, although it is rather differently focused.

FAY, L. E., and EATON, A. T. Instruction in the Use of Books and Libraries: a text-book for normal schools and colleges. 1915. Boston Book Co.

HOPKINS, F. M. Reference Guides that Should be Known and How to Use Them: eight groups of graded lessons in connection with English Courses in high and normal schools. 1916. Detroit: Willard Co.

STEWART, J. D. How to Use a Library. 1910. Elliot Stock.

WARD, G. O. Practical Use of Books and Libraries. 1911. Boston Book Co.

——— Teaching Outline to accompany the Practical Use of Books and Libraries. 1911. Boston Book Co.

CHAPTER XIII

LECTURES

I

The most obvious way to attract children in numbers to a library is by the provision of interesting lectures. These are sometimes called "Library Talks" to mark in part their purpose and in part the quite informal quality that they should as a rule possess. We should have clear views as to the reasons for such lectures; because the librarian must avoid actual general teaching which is the teacher's province; at any rate beyond such teaching as may be given in the use of the library and the care of books. The purpose of the library lecture is to inculcate more successful reading habits; it is not primarily to increase the knowledge of the hearers although that will be also a natural result. Lectures, therefore, should be upon subjects which can be continued in books, and a definite connexion between the subject of the evening and the books on it should be made at every lecture.

Before lectures are decided upon, it must be determined that the library is suitably equipped to give them. The children's room in some libraries, as we have seen, is also a lecture room and can be converted into that character easily and quickly. It is therefore a place with entrances and exits

LECTURES

arranged to meet the conditions prescribed by local authorities for assemblies; has adequate and accessible exits in case of fire or panic and is properly ventilated and lighted. To complete the equipment, it should have electric current available for lantern work, a platform—a movable one is used in some libraries, made up in light sections which can be handled by one person—a lantern screen, which as we have seen may be a blank wall finished in flat white; a lantern, a blackboard, a pointer, and some means of signalling between lecturer and lantern operator. As the ordinary children's room will be part of a library which has equipment for lectures, there is no need here to enlarge greatly upon this subject. It is desirable, however, to say that the most careful attention to every detail of the working of lantern, screens and signals is well worth while, and a lecture given without a hitch makes a happy lecturer and audience.

2

The kind of lectures to be given depends largely upon who is available to give them. Most libraries have little or no money to expend on this work, although there are such notable exceptions as the Liverpool Public Libraries; they are only doubtfully legal under the Public Libraries Acts for the ordinary municipal library. Members of the library staff give lectures in a few libraries, but they cannot run a large number of them and we have to depend upon voluntary lecturers and such lecturers are sometimes difficult to find in smaller towns or in villages. If the librarian is alert they are usually to be found somewhere or other, and there are various lecture societies, working on a national plan, which can be induced to give help. These cannot be specified here, but a few inquiries will reveal at least some of them. The work becomes easier in time: the librarian gradually builds up a whole list of lecturers and organizations who come in to assist. Care must be taken of course that societies which are pushing particular shibboleths are not allowed to use the libraries for their own ends. I have found in experience that a large town has many actual or potential lecturers who can be persuaded to give quite sensible lectures. There are not merely folk who spend an occasional fortnight on the Continent and can describe their experiences, although I have no deep objection to these, if they can be persuaded to confine themselves to the impressionist view of things that they must necessarily possess; but men and women who pursue hobbies, are naturalists, craftsmen, official workers who run important public activities, musicians with some interest in the creative and historic sides of their art, the clergy and ministers many of whom have a favourite subject, and there are many more. If we use the word "talk" instead of lecture part of the difficulty is over. As a matter of fact, an hour's "talk" really requires as much preparation as an hour's "lecture," but the ordinary amateur lecturer does not think so.

LECTURES

Not everybody can lecture to children or can hold their interest. The common virtues of the good lecturer are simplicity, directness and the power of addressing children as equals. Nothing is so foolish, and so disastrous on occasion, as to "talk down" to them. I have seen an audience of over two hundred get quite out of hand because the lecturer simply began with the word "Children!" and crowned his offence by remarking in the next breath: "You children are too young to remember———." This will seem trifling only to those without experience. Involved speaking, the use of words and particularly of ideas beyond ordinary experience—I heard a lecturer describe to ten-year-olds a dam as "the most gargantuan concave monolithic structure in the world"—irony, sarcasm and subtle humour; all these things mean failure blank and total. The difficulty of choosing lecturers, who are voluntary lecturers, who can avoid them, is a matter of experience which is sometimes painful. There is no more keen and penetrating critic within his limits than the child; he goes straight to elemental facts, is intolerant of errors. It is most disconcerting for a lecturer to be corrected on a point of fact by a sharp boy, and this I have seen on occasion.

As for subjects I cannot do better than adapt some words of mine written in 1913, which my later experience has confirmed. The human boy delights in all subjects mechanical—aeroplanes and airships, railways, road transport in all its forms, the telegraph, wireless, the talkies, gramophones: he loves adventures of all types; he will even endure geology if a sufficient number of dinosaurs and pterodactyls add pictorial excitement. The girl, on the other hand, is rather more difficult to interest, although, it is curious to note, she is more regular in her attendance at lectures than he is; even women lecturers prefer to address boys, and when they have a mixed audience do almost invariably devote most of their attention to them; but of course there may be other reasons for this than the mere matter of the amount of response given. But if proof of a girl's utter lack of curiosity as to mechanical contrivances were needed, it could soon be gained by watching a number of girls at a lecture on such a thing as the steam-engine, or even upon the sewing machine. She may *behave* better than the boy, although of late years this cannot be counted on too confidently, but her boredom will be excessive and visible. Literary subjects, biography, history and travel in particular, are of interest to girls. There is a fairly wide range of subjects interesting to boys and girls alike. The tale of travel well told engrosses them; history, some branches of the sciences, particularly the life of the gardens and fields and the simpler aspects of medicine and hygiene, are safe subjects. I have been talking of the average girl and boy. The days that produce an Amy Johnson, women explorers, and women politicians make it clear that there must be some girls who have what used to be considered to be exclusively masculine interests, and as this number

LECTURES

must inevitably increase, such interests should be available for girls in our lectures.

3

Should the lectures be illustrated? This is a question to which the answer is: it depends upon the subject. Concrete subjects, such as the lives of men, mechanical things, places and so on, may assuredly be illustrated with advantage; it is assumed here that the picture is a truthful representation of the thing to be conveyed to the child. Only a good lecturer can draw a verbal picture of a battlefield, or a piece of mechanism, and certainly few or none can convey the idea of a man or woman to a child. The objection, therefore, that slides interrupt lectures, is outweighed by the advantages they give. On the other hand pictures illustrating works of imagination are usually to be deprecated as they replace the child's own vivid imagination by someone else's. Twenty good slides used in a lecture lasting an hour are enough as a rule; too many slides make a bad lecture. Moreover, they should be handled carefully both by lecturer and operator. Otherwise effects little expected occur, as, in the one kind, when a lecturer, bent on illustrating the horrors of the Colosseum, showed *The Christians to the Lions*, and heard a small voice pipe out, "Mother, look; there's a poor lion that hasn't got a Christian"; and, in the other kind, such a *contretemps* as happened years ago at Stepney when a lecturer beginning his lecture on Queen Victoria thus: "We will now look upon our late beloved sovereign in her usual attitude of reposeful dignity" was confronted immediately after with the portrait of the Queen on the screen—upside down! The lecturer, too, must be prepared for the buzz of interested comment which in all but well-drilled audiences greets the appearance of a new slide, and must "wait for it."

As the availability or otherwise of slides will often determine whether a lecture can be given or not, some libraries build up a collection of slides; some have members of staff who make them occasionally for special subjects. In Croydon, for example, the libraries possess 15,000 slides which have been acquired by making, purchase and generous gifts. There are circulating libraries of slides a subscription with which will procure many useful sets, and these have catalogues from which they may be selected. In recent years this matter of the pictorial illustration of lectures has been helped greatly by the perfecting of the epidiascope which may now be bought at a reasonable cost, although a good one is beyond the means of small children's libraries. This is an instrument which by means of mirrors and lenses will throw upon a screen a picture of an actual object or a picture direct from a book or print with the clearness of an ordinary lantern slide. At present it is hardly suitable for large rooms as the "throw" is less than forty feet and is really effective at twenty-five or thirty. Unless the floor

LECTURES

is raked upwards from platform to back of room the instrument gets in the way of the audience. In a small room it makes a display of illustrations possible in the readiest way, and every librarian can see the great economy and special effectiveness of such a machine.

Modern public libraries have separate lecture rooms in which their lectures for children are held. While they have the disadvantage of taking children out of the actual children's department, it is possible in them to have more adequate equipment. The most recent have cinema installations, and I think the film can be definitely valuable here. There are simple projection machines and non-flammable films on large numbers of subjects and on representations of classic stories and plays which the librarian can use to advantage. Here, however, the questions of a projecting room, precautions against fire and problems of selection arise which must be given careful thought. The library must not expect to compete with the commercial cinema with its unlimited resources and varieties of appeal; but something it can do, while showing subjects which increase reading, to give children a type of film which would not always be profitable in the programme of the cinema itself.

4

Forethought in arranging the audience is advisable. Usually the number of children who wish to attend lectures outruns the accommodation considerably, and admission by ticket is the rule. Such tickets are distributed at the library or through the schools or through both. As we desire to attract more children to become library users, the balance will be kept between regular users and others. The tickets should be simple and can be produced by duplicator, and may bear on them a few well-chosen titles on the subject of the lecture. Private schools should not be forgotten in the distribution. About 10 per cent. over the accommodation can be allowed for tickets that will not be used, but not when the scheme is new; all are used then. Teachers may be asked how many tickets they can use, and they may also be asked not to make them rewards for good behaviour in school—but this must be done tactfully!

So simple a matter as the day and hour will be carefully considered, in view of the school and other engagements of the child. There should be an interval for tea between school and lecture, if it is on ordinary week-day evenings. I have found six in the evening to be a good hour. Saturday mornings are sometimes chosen, but less frequently of recent years as children ought to be at play when the hours are light. The ideal length of a lecture is fifty minutes; in any case it should not exceed an hour, as children cannot be expected to keep still for longer. Indeed adult lectures would be more effective than they usually are were they so limited.

Audiences are of both sexes as a rule; but it is sometimes advisable to give a different evening to

LECTURES

each sex. When they are mixed it is perhaps wise to give one part of the room to boys and another to girls. Local experience may settle this, but my own suggests such separation. Punctuality should be insisted upon as every newcomer after a lecture has begun distracts the whole audience. During the proceedings silence is essential and should be demanded. The desire for sweets, chewing gum and nuts should be suppressed, and at the end of the lecture it is a good plan to get the girls away well before the boys. Instructions embodying these requirements may be written on lantern slides and thrown on the screen. If the discipline is kindly and firmly maintained at the outset, the audiences soon learn to keep it. Unless it can be maintained lectures should not be attempted.

5

The gramophone can be used to advantage in talks and demonstrations of various kinds, as when talks on music, folk-songs and similar matters are given. I have not found it necessary to provide one, but occasionally one has been borrowed or hired. As for wireless, there is little doubt that libraries should make what use of it they can; there may be something in the Children's Hour, or an occasional lecture at suitable times, which can be received, but the talks of most value to children are given for schools in school hours and are therefore not available for libraries which are not in schools. There is, for these reasons, no possibility of arranging the listening groups for children which are common for adults; but, of course, the present hours of broadcasts may not always be maintained. Clearly, unless there is a separate "story-hour" room which can be devoted wholly to such purposes, these aids can only be employed on organized occasions. The noise of either at other times would be a distraction from reading and would defeat the purposes of the library.

6

The children's librarian cannot be expected to be a lecturer: that is to say, it is not exactly an essential part of library ability to be one. The object of this chapter is to deal with the arrangement of lectures by non-librarians. Nevertheless, it is a great convenience to be able to give an occasional lecture on the library or its contents; to be competent to fill the gaps which occur in the most carefully planned programmes. Story-telling—an activity requiring slightly different gifts—is a part of the librarian's equipment, and I would assert that the ability to make a coherent speech is necessary to modern librarians; and the lecture is only an extension of this after all. It may thus be useful to add a few very simple hints on lecturing drawn from a somewhat lengthy experience with many types of child audience. The underlying principles are the same whatever that audience may be.

Prepare the lecture carefully with a beginning,

LECTURES

an objective and a conclusion. A beginner is wise to write out the lecture and then to lose the manuscript on the day it is to be delivered; the act of writing impresses the matter sufficiently on the memory in most cases. Before writing, a list of the headings should have been made in order to ensure coherence and completeness, and in the end this outline may serve as your notes. It is better, however, to be without even notes, for your own experience as a hearer will tell you how much you preferred being talked to to being read to in any way; and a preoccupation with notes means a loss of touch with the audience which fails to get the best response from it. Practice your lecture; hear the sound of your own voice in empty rooms, or in a wood if you can find one where an unexpected audience may not rise in startled doubt of your sanity; recite it quietly on your solitary walks. Don't despise these methods which the greatest speakers have employed. In a short time your lecture will become a part of you; there will be no stuttering failure of words and no lame and impotent conclusion—or variety of conclusions, for a bad lecturer or speaker always seems to have several natural endings to a speech and not to realize the fact.

When you go upon a platform don't be in too great a hurry to begin. *Don't say anything until the audience, which of course has been chattering volubly, is quiet.* Then begin slowly, deliberately and in a subdued voice, not with the yell which some elocutionists think is the best opening; and in the first few sentences keep clear of any fact or statement which is crucial, because, however much we try, the children are usually not receptive for a moment or two. Modulate your voice to the room and be sure that the children at the back hear you. This is achieved by pitch, not by shouting; a treble voice carries much farther than a low one. Don't clip your words or drop your tone at the end of sentences. This fault, to which those who read or who depend upon notes are specially prone, may ruin the best of speeches.

A lecturer who talks against a talking audience is lost. Perfect silence cannot be expected unless there is a perfect lecturer. If the lecture is in any way dull, tedious, or badly given, the children first lose interest, then begin to fidget and from thence to talking and disorder is only a short distance. But it is reasonable to expect some courtesy and patience even from the youngsters; and although we must admit that uneasiness in children is a symptom of boredom, of an attempt on their part to gain distraction from the annoying or dull proceedings with which they ought to be occupied, attention should be insisted upon. To keep perfectly cool, to be completely master of the audience, are essentials, to stop dead immediately any talking is heard.

The greatest source of annoyance is the habitual discussion which arises whenever a new slide appears. The lecturer should halt immediately, however interesting the matter in hand may be. Careless youngsters, chattering recklessly, are galvanized into silence when in a pause they find their voices soaring in the sudden quiet; nothing is more effective in renewing attention. Similar results can be obtained by raising or lowering the tone, or altering the speed of speaking; but these are methods to be learned only by experience. Children are fairly indulgent to nervous lecturers, providing their matter is interesting. Of the signals by which change of slides is indicated, the castanet is the worst form. Usually the lecturer holds it behind his back and snaps it when a new slide is wanted; often through muscular nervousness snaps it at wrong times, and at the best it is a distraction, as the children jump every time it is used. The best signal is a word or phrase agreed between lecturer and lanternist. Other methods are a very muffled buzzer or electric bell, which only the lanternist can hear, or a light which flashes where only he can see it, which can be pressed from the platform. Another method, but somewhat doubtful because theatrical, is the drawing of the pointer at a given diagonal across the screen.

It will be seen that many trifles have been included here, but it is often on little things that the success or failure of a lecture depends, and this chapter is not written for experts.

7

Finally, there is the connecting up of the lecture with books. I have already suggested that titles may be given on the backs of the tickets of admission.

Various other ways will commend themselves. Where there is room for their examination the books may be displayed on tables at the lecture, and the children can be allowed to borrow them then and there. Lists may be thrown on the screen. Lantern slides with a writing surface can be obtained at any photographic chemist which can be used for this work, but they are rather expensive. Ordinary lantern slide cover glasses, which can be bought for a few pence a dozen, if sponged over with a 1-per-cent. solution of photographic gelatine in warm water and allowed to dry, will take ink-writing quite well, and of course can be washed and used again and again. Other methods for bringing lecture and book together will no doubt commend themselves to an ingenious librarian, and it can never be too often repeated that this is our first as it is our final purpose.

AUTHORITIES

BROWN, J. D. Manual of Library Economy. Chap. 34—The Lecture Room. 1931. Grafton.

McCOLVIN, L. R. Library Extension Work. Chap. 3—Lectures, and Chap. 4—Library Work with Children. 1927. Grafton.

Books on voice production and the speaking art are many. Those I have used—but there are many others—are Elsie Fogerty's *Speech Craft*, 1930 (Dent); Harold Ford's *Art of Extempore Speaking*, 1898 (Elliot Stock); John Hullah's *The Cultivation of the Speaking Voice*, 1884 (Clarendon Press); and J. H. Williams's *Voice Production and Breathing for Speakers*, 1923 (Pitman).

CHAPTER XIV

THE STORY HOUR

I

The telling of stories is an invaluable, and it may be argued an essential, activity of the well-organized children's library. Those of us whose childhood reaches to Victorian days have recollections of the fireside telling of stories, before motor-car, cinema and wireless provided their more exciting but probably less useful substitutes. In some homes the reading and telling of stories continues, but they are fewer than they were. The loss is great, as it was here that the child was most appropriately introduced to his fairylands. Stories in schools and libraries are a substitute only, but they have also rather different aims. Amusement was the end of the fireside stories although other advantages accrued. In the school the story is meant to develop qualities: imagination, knowledge of English, dramatic joy in fine action, and so on; the end is educational. As such stories are told in schools, why duplicate the work in libraries? Because the aim in the latter is to open books which might not otherwise be known; it is not to teach or to improve in the accepted sense of these words.

The Story Hour at the Ashburton Library, Croydon

2

This was the reason for library lectures, and the condition applies that stories which are an end in themselves and cannot be found in books, are hardly the type for our work. I doubt if such books as the many collections we have with such titles as *Stories for the Story Hour*, consisting of original stories, or stories which cannot be followed up, are really useful in libraries. A child can read such stories easily himself. What we want as our ideal are stories based on great books which will create the desire to read those books. Much modern so-called story-telling is time wasted from the library point of view. It is wise, however, to be fairly elastic, as the telling of one story from what may be called an artificial collection, may introduce the collection when it is new. Lamb's *Tales from Shakespeare*, and Kingsley's *Heroes* in a lesser degree, are types of ideal "treatment," as we cannot imagine any child who has been made familiar with Lamb's *Tales* who would not want sooner or later to read Shakespeare himself.

The story hour,—which need not last an hour, but the term is convenient,—is a more intimate affair than a lecture. The conditions are to be as unconstrained and simple as possible. The group to which it is told should not exceed about thirty children, and is better if it is smaller. This is difficult where the demand exceeds what can reasonably be done, but story-telling to hundreds at a time is something that has passed out of the sphere of the librarian into that of the entertainer. Imagine such an audience listening to one of the *Just So Stories*, and then descending upon the library with demands for the book itself, as should be the result if the story is rightly told! It merely makes the library an irritation to children. A story party should be a sort of family gathering with intimate touch between teller and hearer.

It is customary to give stories to quite small children as well as to older ones, and a different sort of story for each. Fairy tales and legends from folk lore are the basis of those for the tinies. For older children the "hours" may be made roughly systematic; and to them may be given connected stories from the Greek writers, from Indian folk lore and literature, from Dante, from the literature of travel, and so on; the choice is infinite.

3

The ideal way of giving a story hour would be to stop the work of the library as such with, "Now we will have a story," and to tell it. So we should get informality. But in busy libraries that is impossible, as all the children cannot spare time for or do not want the story; they merely want to read or to borrow a book for home reading. Thus, it has become the rule to have the story at times when the library is not doing its lending or reference work: or a special room is used, as we saw when we were discussing the planning of such libraries. Formality, indeed, so far enters into our arrangements that even the day and hour at which stories will be told are announced beforehand, and some librarians have been driven to the use of tickets in order to keep the audiences within limits. The story corner, or room, should be cosy, with a fireplace, a chair for the teller and a mat on which little ones can sit. The formation of the group is a semi-circle about the fire beside which the teller sits; the fire may be one of the electrical imitation fires with a flicker which are so successful to-day. Sometimes an effect is added if the lights are shaded in subdued colours, at a cost of a few pence.

4

There are natural story-tellers as we know from everyday experience, but those to whom the gift was not bestowed by the birth fairies may become passable substitutes and most of us must be content to be that. Training in story-telling is part of the Froebel course, and in America special instruction is given.[1] There is not much of it available for librarians in England, but there are helpful books.

[1] In Croydon our children's librarians and such assistants as show any aptitude for work with children are each given an elementary course in voice production, diction, and story-telling, by a professional teacher of elocution (Miss Kathleen Rich, editor of *A Playground of Poems*, Methuen, 1931) whom the Libraries' Committee engages for the purpose. The results have been quite good. Miss Lillian H. Smith, head of the Toronto children's department, finds such teaching "regrettable," but I feel that it is justified except in the case of the born story-teller. If the pattern is a good one, it does not really matter if we all conform to it.

THE STORY HOUR

Careful study of a story well repays itself, because it is an ill-service to present a garbled version of a masterpiece. Learn it by heart by all means, if that is your only way of securing verbal facility, but then make sure that you have the spirit of the thing and are able to avoid a sing-song delivery in which the drama which is in all good stories is smothered. I think it better to know, not the words, but the natural sequence of the story thoroughly, and to tell it in words adapted to the audience; this is less affected and more effective. A story should be told continuously, without interruption for explanations, pauses to ask questions, or attempt to inculcate a moral. Question-asking is destructive, Miss Marie Shedlock gives an example of the story-teller who began thus, "An old lady looked out of her window one morning, and what do you think she saw?"

The answer from the imagination of the child, which was of course far more active than her own, was—

"Please, mum, an elephant!"

The teller's crestfallen "No, it was a little kitten," was a miserable collapse which ought to have been avoided. As for the moral, no child or anyone else objects to it if it is provided by the story, but stories told for the sake of a moral fail of that and every other purpose. Our moral as librarians, if one may use the word in this way, is that the book from which our story is drawn is a good one not to be neglected by our hearers without loss of something really jolly. The teller should have a copy or copies at

A MANUAL OF CHILDREN'S LIBRARIES

some of the story hours and should show it to the children, and, if possible, even invite them to take it then and there.

AUTHORITIES

CATHER, K. D. Educating by Story-Telling. 1919. Harrap.
HAZELTINE, ALICE I., (Ed.). Library Work with Children, pp. 273–316. *Classics of Amer. Librarianship.* 1917. N.Y.: Wilson Co.
PARTRIDGE, E. N. and G. E. Story-Telling in the School and Home. 1913. N.Y.: Sturgis & Walton.
SHEDLOCK, MARIE L. Art of Story-Telling. 1915.
—— The Story-Telling Art. National Sunday School Union.

Many articles will be found in library journals

CHAPTER XV

READINGS, DRAMATIC READINGS AND PLAYER CLUBS

I

Readings from books are worth while where story-telling is not done, or as a variation even where it is; and have exactly the same objects as story-telling. This work must be done after study to get the best results, because it requires an even greater effort of attention on the part of the children. Fair results, however, can be obtained by any average reader; I have known, who has not? older children read to younger ones with great acceptance. Such reading is particularly useful when, as happened when *Winnie-the-Pooh* appeared, the demand for a book is too great for any library to supply enough copies. In that case by reading it aloud to groups, many children were introduced to the doings of Pooh and Piglet who might have had to wait a very long time otherwise. Voluntary helpers can be induced to read who would be alarmed at requests to tell stories. Of course all the conditions as to choice of books to be read, numbers of hearers and duration of the reading apply as in the case of story hours.

2

Somewhat different are the dramatic readings which have become rather common in late years. Here a play of merit is chosen. Each child has a copy of it, and is cast for a part exactly as if it were to be played, and the play is read from the book each reader taking up his cues as if he were acting. A little acting is sometimes introduced, but that is unnecessary, and may injure the general effect, which is really remarkable at times. A play well read gives the illusion of actual acting and may even get the meaning of the writer over to certain audiences better than actual acting. In the first place such readings are pursued for the joy they give to their readers, but, with the necessary number of rehearsals, parties may read to the library audiences with success.

3

From this it is only a step to the actual acting of plays. This is done nowadays and there is much to be said for it, if it is within the power of the staff, if the general conditions are right, and if there is enough voluntary assistance. The producing of a play in costume does not call for elaborate stage equipment, but curtains that move easily, a platform, retiring places for exits and entrances, simple lighting effects, and music from piano or gramophone. It also means many hours of preparation in the designing of costumes, making of simple

READINGS AND PLAYER CLUBS

scenery, and in rehearsal. The actual choice of a play is no simple matter,—although there are versions, quite playable by young folks, of *Dick Whittington*, *Cinderella* and *Rip van Winkle* stories,—because many plays must be studied before one suitable for the place and to the attainments of the available young players is found. With these necessary cautions, which are meant to suggest that this work may seriously interfere with the scanty leisure of the librarian and impede what I regard as the real work of the library, one may say that there is much in favour of establishing clubs of children players. In one library a skilful professional actor undertook for some years to run one drawn from the children. Every dress and property was home-made, and the results were remarkable. Although every library cannot expect to find such expert help easily, the notes of the producer on his aims will be suggestive.

The past year has seen the launching of a dramatic club among the children—the Junior Library Players.

The policy in forming its method of work has been one that draws attention, by careful planning and production, to the calls that every well-arranged play makes, at some time or other, upon practically every known art or craft—to mention Poetry, Literature, Music, Elocution, Line, Perspective, Colour-combining, Grouping (Plastic Arts), Gesture and rhythmic Movement, Costume, and the design and manufacture of appropriate "properties" and accessories, is by no means to exhaust the list.

The Club had on loan a home-made, but efficient Radio Gramophone with three loud-speakers—one behind the scenes and two in the auditorium with a change-over switch —and by means of this device, suitable music of the finest and most varied character could be broadcast from any make of gramophone record. In this way, at a recent performance of *Dick Whittington*, the audience was enabled to hear the *actual voice* of Bow Bells playing the traditional "Whittington Chimes."

In the "putting-over" of a play the young actors are expected to characterize, and to speak out clearly, and with *natural inflections*. All colourless and affected "elocutionary" graces are strongly discouraged. . . . It is insisted that a play is team work—that one plays for one's side (i.e. Club)—that throughout the production it is not just a question of "my part," but of "my part" in relation to "our play." That the children have been quick to grasp these essentials of good workmanship is apparent in the care they give to the rendering of small parts. Early in the rehearsals it could be clearly seen that each player, however humble his or her part might be, realized a perfect rendering of that part to be essential to the complete effect of the play as a whole.

A pleasing success has attended the work, and our audiences have expressed keen appreciation of the vigour and spontaneity of the acting and the balance and harmony of the production.

4

Reading and discussion circles, or literary clubs are another activity. These groups, as is the case with all the clubs or circles formed in libraries, have their own organizations, and elect their own officers, who may be a leader and a secretary, or one individual who combines both functions; and are only supervised by the librarian. A book is chosen by vote which should in the view of the librarian be worth the time it is proposed to expend upon it; selected passages are read before each meeting; and sometimes

READINGS AND PLAYER CLUBS

papers are written upon it which open the discussion of those passages. These circles have been most successful in some places, but only where good leaders are available; otherwise the interest fades long before the season ends. A new leader is sometimes elected for each meeting but this presumes a fairly high average of ability in the group. Sometimes a grown-up acts as leader, but, good as this is, it is not so satisfactory as when the children lead themselves.

5

In our limits of space it is impossible to describe or even to mention every detail of the many activities that rise naturally in a live library. Clubs for stamp collecting and discussion, and for the examination of wild flowers that have been gathered between meetings, are examples of the many things which add variety and interest, and make demands upon the qualities, physical and other, of the librarian.

AUTHORITIES

Most of the material here is drawn from personal observation. Articles on clubs, reading circles, etc., will be found by consulting the indexes of library journals; there is no monograph on the subject. Conelly Richards's *Two Plays*, Dent, 1931, has an introduction giving his methods of production, which were those he employed at Croydon.

CHAPTER XVI

EXHIBITIONS, ILLUSTRATION COLLECTIONS

I

Displays of various sorts can be made for which the word exhibition is perhaps too grandiose. These may consist of the showing of particular books in racks or tables with labels such as "Books the Librarian has read and recommends." "Christmas Books," "Men of Your Own Town," and so on without limit. There may be displays of books on lecture subjects drawn from all parts of a library system as is usual in the Bristol libraries. There are sometimes exhibitions which are of a "museum" character, on local fauna and flora. "The dolls of all nations" is another example which was used effectively to draw attention to costume and travel books. Such exhibitions can be very elaborate, with objects displayed in glass cases and meticulously labelled, and these can be undertaken when funds and conditions permit; but in this, as in everything connected with the library, only as they serve and do not impede the issue and study of books, should such things be undertaken. I have known hours to be spent on posters, labels and so on which were beautiful in their way, but meant the neglect of definite library work. The danger lies in the fact

EXHIBITIONS

that we may become too engrossed in such work and pursue it until our sense of values is damaged. There is no doubt that book-display is to be a feature of future librarianship. The library should be the centre to which people come for impartial advice about the choice of books; and exhibitions for a month before Christmas of books really suitable for presents are examples of work that a library may do.

2

Akin to the activities we have described is the collecting and preserving of illustrations. It is now the custom to examine all discarded books, periodicals, catalogues, prospectuses and other illustrated materials for pictures which in the ordinary way are destroyed; to cut them out, mount and file them. In this manner there is built up in course of time a veritable encyclopædia of illustrations, of the utmost value for exhibition in the children's library in connexion with anniversaries or current topics, and to teachers for use in class work.

Such a collection may be made with the help of children, who cut out and mount pictures as a pastime. The illustrations should be of some factual value, illustrating definite things. For example, a picture of a rose, if it is one of a recognizable variety, is a useful thing, because in time one may get illustrations of all the family; but a pretty picture of flowers in a vase, unless it is chosen as an example of a special school of art, is valueless in our collec-

Mounting Illustrations

tion; similarly, pools with paddling cows reflected in them, pretty woodland scenes which might be in Hampshire or in Gloucestershire, and unidentifiable sea-scapes, are examples that we do not want. What we do want are pictures of historical events and places, portraits, animal pictures, birds, individual trees, flowers and grasses, inventions, industrial processes, mechanisms, varieties of transport and so on: all definitely pictures of something.

The pictures are cut out and trimmed, and then mounted on nature-paper mounts. The librarian, if she does not do the actual work of cutting out, must make final choice of the illustrations, on the principle that it is better to build slowly and carefully than to get a great collection of inferior material. On the other hand, the value of the collection depends in some measure on its size; for example, one picture of St. Paul's Cathedral is useful, but a series showing its exterior, interior, monuments and ornamentation from every point of view, may supplement verbal accounts in a way that everyone can understand. Such a collection in connexion with the epidiascope suggests many possibilities. The nature-paper mounts can be purchased from the firms which specialize in book-cover papers; they should be fairly thick but not quite inflexible, of colours that throw up the somewhat cold pictures we have sometimes to use, and that will wear well and not show finger-marks too plainly. I have found sage green and vandyck brown to be useful colours, but taste may well differ on this matter. The sizes I use myself

EXHIBITIONS

are for ordinary pictures approximately 12½ inches by 10½ inches, and for larger pictures 17 inches by 13¼ inches. Two sizes are generally sufficient, and many more of the smaller will be wanted than of the larger. There is no need to buy stocks of mounts for very large pictures: they can be dealt with individually if need arise, but it is a good policy to confine the collection to those which will go on the two standard sizes.

Illustrations are mounted with a good, acid-free paste, and should dry under light pressure in a letter press or under weights. Care must be taken that each illustration has a clearly-descriptive title or much will be lost. The illustrations are now classified by the same system as the books, the class-mark being written on the right-hand top corner of the mount. They are then filled. There are two or three ways of doing this. I prefer to file the smaller and more numerous illustrations in steel vertical filing cabinets exactly as if they were classified cards, with projecting guide cards. This, provided the classification used is the Dewey Decimal, with the index to that system, makes a readily accessible collection. These files cannot always be afforded, and a cheaper method is to file them in boxes. Fincham's boxes[1] are excellent, the specification of which is: a cardboard illustration box to lie flat on shelf, made with lid and hinged front, covered on the outside with marbled paper (or cloth: specify colour desired) and inside with white paper. A xylonite label holder to

[1] A. A. Fincham, Spa Works, Northampton Row, E.C.

be attached to the narrow end. The inside measurements to be 13 inches long by 10¾ inches wide and 3⅝ inches deep. Other sizes can of course be ordered to the size of the mount used, but ¼-inch "play" must be allowed in making the inside measurements. Such filing boxes, or "transfer cases" as they are called, can be obtained in steel from Libraco and other file-making firms.

The uses of these illustrations are many; for exhibitions on the screens with lists of books for wall decoration in story hours and so on; but they also have a large use for schools. Teachers are allowed to borrow them in batches of from fifty to illustrate lessons. When this is done a simple cloth-board portfolio should be provided in which they can safely be carried to and from the library.

AUTHORITIES

DANA, J. C. Modern Library Economy. Pt. 5—(3), Picture Collection. 1917. Woodstock, Vermont, U.S.A.: Elm Tree Press.

WHEELER, J. L. The Library and the Community. 1924. Chicago: A.L.A.

Many articles are to be found in library journals, especially American ones.

CHAPTER XVII

PUBLICITY AND PUBLICATIONS AND THE RELATIONSHIPS OF THE LIBRARY

1

Good relations will be cultivated with all whom the library serves. These begin conveniently with the teachers and parents, as these pages must have suggested. Where it is possible the librarian should have the closest relations with the teachers, and it is a good principle "to go and see rather than to write." Visits should, circumstances allowing, be paid to every school once a term. These visits need not be long, and should ostensibly be to afford the teacher a chance of saying in what further ways the library may serve him or his school. The teacher must have special consideration always, be provided with any books or pictures or other library material necessary for his personal work; and the children's librarian is the best person to draw out those needs.

2

In the schools a board can usually be displayed with information concerning the libraries and new book jackets. Most teachers will keep a stock of vouchers which they hand to children who may benefit by the use of the libraries. These are fairly obvious ways of mutual help. Occasionally the children's librarian may be invited to address classes in the school on some subject connected with her work. In the last year of their school life all children should be brought to the library to receive the lesson in how to use it which is set out in Chapter XII; and this and all other "library lessons" are arranged on these school visits. Some librarians, as in Leeds, address a letter, signed by the director of education and the chief librarian, to every school leaver, which is accompanied by a voucher of admission to the libraries, in which the youngster is asked persuasively to continue his education by the various means the library offers. Although this is a little past the children's librarian's work, she is again, I think, the best person to arrange the distribution of such letters through the teachers.

3

At intervals conferences with the teachers collectively should take place. These are most conveniently held at meetings of the Teacher's Association, and there experience and ideas may be pooled and discussed on many matters; amongst them the reactions of reading on children, the provision of certain types of books, such as re-written classics, abridged editions, works in clipped English and in dialect, as well as the means of more effective library service. Such meetings of this kind as I have

PUBLICITY AND PUBLICATIONS

arranged have been very fruitful. Teachers, although busy people faced with the exacting demands of modern examinations, will often give definite direct help in the libraries, in arranging exhibitions, taking story hours, choosing and preparing illustrations, and in other ways. Mutual exchange of assistance must be of great advantage.

4

In the parent the librarian will find her other best coadjutor; at least in more cases, although we have known parents who have no interest in what their children read. It is well to cultivate the view that the parents are all-important; that they are welcome in the library at all times and especially at hours when the children are absent and when the librarian can talk to them. They should be encouraged to watch over the books their children take; even to read them. Mothers of very little children should be encouraged to borrow books to read to them. The criticisms, suggestions and advice of parents should be invited and welcomed. They should learn to regard the library as a place where they may feel at home and in which they have a definite stake— as indeed they must have if their children mean anything to them. The children's librarian can often bring parents who are not readers to become such. We do know that children themselves are the best library missionaries to grown-ups.

A good plan is to have at intervals a Parents'

Evening. Christmas is a good time, in connexion with the story-hour festivals some of us organize at that season. Here the dramatic club can play to them: or stories, as usual in the Story Hour, be told; or a lantern lecture be given; and in an interval the librarian can welcome them, and tell them of what is being done for their children. Several adaptations of this idea will occur to every librarian.

5

Other publicity work of various kinds is undertaken. The most ambitious is the magazine. In 1922 Croydon issued a *Junior Library News*, and in the next year the charming children's library in Paris, "L'Heure Joyeuse," put forth a similar periodical. These were produced on the duplicator, the Croydon edition being 3,000 copies monthly. In 1929 Leeds issued an attractive printed bulletin for children, called *The Chimney Corner*, and Hendon followed in 1930, with *The Magic Casement*, on similar lines. The Croydon *Junior Library News* is now issued in printed form every two months. These magazines contain announcements of library events, articles on writers for children (i.e. Carroll, Henty, Farrar, Kipling, etc.), and notes on the seasons and anniversaries, and similar matters, written with the aim of drawing attention to the bearing of books upon them. They contain, too, lists of the additions of books with notes.

PUBLICITY AND PUBLICATIONS

6

Further publicity may be gained by the use of the screens in the junior library for posting topical illustrations, birthday portraits, etc., with selected and purposely very brief lists of books. Reading lists or book-marks bearing titles of books which for special reasons the librarian wishes to advertise can be produced quite easily if there is a subject catalogue and a duplicator. For the largest libraries the printed list is accessible seeing that some of them have a printery attached, and some have the Gammeter installed. An electrically-driven duplicating machine will turn out over 1,000 copies an hour and is to be recommended for large libraries which cannot face the expense of printing. Hand rotary duplicators must serve in smaller libraries: and for the smallest the flat machine will do: indeed I find the very best work is done on the flat machine. Lists should be issued while the subject is vivid in the children's minds; should anticipate rather than follow demand.

7

The chief relationship of the children's library is with the adult library. The lessons which are outlined in Chapter XII are intended to result in the youngsters becoming life-long library users. In practice it occurs only too often that when they reach school-leaving age they actually come to the library with the remark: "I'm leaving school; I shan't want any more books." Here then is a problem which can be dealt with from the very beginning of a library career if the suggestion is always kept to the front that books are not for a part of life only. One practical way of retaining the adolescent is the "intermediate library," as it is sometimes called. Where conditions have allowed it success has followed, to some extent at least. This library is often only a set of shelves, but it is better if it is a separate room, in which are kept books and periodicals which appeal to the middle and later teens.

Good books on the professions, all fields of office work and management, the trades and industries, travel, history and biography; and the works of the novelists which lads and girls are known to prefer, such as Buchan, Haggard, Mason, the better detective writers from Doyle to (yes) Edgar Wallace, Wells, as well as the classic novelists. Such a library must be open to later hours than the ordinary children's library; in fact until about 8.30 or 9 in the evenings and on Saturday afternoons and evenings, or at such hours as local knowledge dictates. It must be staffed.

The librarian must be familiar with the resources of all departments of the libraries in which she serves. She will find her pride in the fact that her readers, after school-life, remain attached readers. She will see that at the appropriate time every one of them is properly introduced to the adult library and given the freedom of it.

PUBLICITY AND PUBLICATIONS
AUTHORITIES

Material on the subjects treated has not been incorporated into monographs, but there is much to be found in the library journals. On publicity work in general, Lionel R. McColvin's *Library Extension Work*; Gilbert O. Ward's *Publicity for Public Libraries* (1924. N.Y.: Wilson Co.); and Joseph L. Wheeler's *The Library and the Community* are to be recommended; and for current doings see the Library Association's *The Year's Work in Librarianship* (Vol. I, 1928, and continuations), and the American Library Association's *Children's Library Year Book* (Vol. I, 1929, and continuations).

CHAPTER XVIII

SCHOOL LIBRARIES: GENERAL

I

It would be beyond my scope in this book to attempt to give a full account of School libraries, their activities, and the possibilities which librarians see in them. Quite clearly, however, a book on children's libraries which ignored them would be very incomplete. There are several types of school and libraries are essential to every one of them; a fact not yet adequately realized, although the subject has received more attention in recent years, as may be gathered from *The Report of the Consultative Committee of the Board of Education on Books in Public Elementary Schools* which was published by the Stationery Office in 1928. But it is instructive to note, as showing how far the authorities are from really understanding the possibilities of a library, that amongst the twenty persons who sat for two years to produce this report not one was a librarian.

All wise education leads sooner or later to the right use of books; that is to say, employs them as tools, checks on experience, means of research. If we are told that books are not life or education but a substitute for one and an aid to the other, we accept the platitude with the remark that it is a poor excuse for neglecting what is in fact the main means of transmitting man's experiences here on earth. Usually the phrase is as hypocritical as, in the larger sense, it is untrue. How far does the elementary school teach definite research in history, literature and indeed in most subjects? Some efforts in the direction are made, but they cannot be successful in any measure when there are inadequate libraries or none at all in which to make them. Teachers are alive to the fact if some of their authorities are not. The time is foreshadowed, however, when every school will have a library of books which illustrate every subject in the school curriculum; and it may take two forms: a general library for the school as a whole, in which there will be the greater reference books; and there may be form libraries adapted to the attainments of the pupils. (In mentioning "reference books" it may be useful to remind teachers that the term really means books such as encyclopædias, atlases, dictionaries, etc., which are consulted for individual facts and are not read through; it does not mean non-fictional books merely, although these may be used as reference books. For example, *The Dictionary of National Biography* is a reference book, but Macaulay's *History of England* is not.)

2

Teachers are not librarians, although they may be so called, unless they have been through a course of training in librarianship. This, again, is not yet sufficiently realized, and at present the Board of Education does not recognize the librarian in the schools; but I believe that this is something we may expect to be changed before long. As a rule teachers undertake the work, and if they do it well they have little time left for teaching. This is, perhaps, more true in secondary schools, because in them actual research work and information finding are or ought to be essential. The Board of Education itself has issued the statement that "a library is no less an indispensible part of every secondary school than a laboratory." The same statement goes on: "The school library serves two purposes, study and general recreative reading. If the pupil is to do his work intelligently, he must have at hand, and learn to read and use, a number of books which bear directly on his studies; it is also very desirable that he should cultivate a taste for more general reading; and by reading books on many subjects develop breadth of view and catholicity of interest."

A school library should be in a separate room, accessible at all times to teachers and their classes, because some of its value will be in the "laboratory" work done there as part of school studies. The new school should have such a room always, but everyone recognizes how difficult it is to find one in an older school. The memorandum already quoted suggests that where space is available "the erection of a building of light construction may be possible," and continues, "sometimes a room which might be thought unlikely can be adapted, for often the very irregularity in shape which may make the room unsuitable for other purposes will provide recesses appropriate to a library." Certainly such a room is better than none; indeed the further suggestion that ordinary class-rooms or the assembly hall, where there is one, may be shelved as a library is right in this sense. But odd-shaped rooms present difficulties in the way of standard shelving and furniture, which ought to be as right for a school as for any other library. Until the authorities plan and budget for proper school libraries the wise teacher will make the best of what opportunities he gets; indeed he does do this; but I think it should be said in a manual such as this, that such planning and such budgeting, now occasional, will be universal before very long.

3

The equipment, cataloguing, classification and general arrangements of a school library resemble those in the ordinary children's library; and the methods I have already described suffice for most cases. Where furniture—shelves and tables—can be made in the manual classes of the schools it should conform to the orthodox librarian's measurements for the simple reason that experience shows them to be the most suitable and economical.

For the book stock of the library the Board of Education has made a series of useful suggestions.[1]

[1] Memorandum on Libraries in State-aided Secondary Schools, 1928.

The actual management in secondary schools is usually a committee consisting of the Head Teacher and about two of his assistants and two boys. In some schools the committee is a larger one; and the members are often called the "school librarians." The actual librarian may be a teacher or a sixth form pupil; but if the library is a large one and the librarian has other work than that of the library to do, there must be a rota of librarians with its necessarily attendant difficulties. "Much depends upon the librarian, who needs to have not only a sense of order but a wide knowledge of books. He will himself be a book-lover, and his influence should be felt not only in the pupil's choice of books but in the attractiveness of the library and the facilities for its use."

This committee makes rules as to hours of service, the treatment of books, the charging of those that are lent, fines and penalties; and its most important work is to buy new books and discard old ones if necessary. The rules should be as liberal as the welfare of the library permits. It should be open all the school day and for some time after each session, and the pupils should have free access to the shelves. Borrowing should be permitted except in the case of books which may be required almost simultaneously by a whole form. In holidays this borrowing may be allowed more freely than during term.

SCHOOL LIBRARIES—GENERAL

4

Our attention has been directed to the secondary school in the last page or two, but obviously most of the points have importance for the elementary and even the higher school; indeed for all schools public or private. Elementary teachers, where there is not a public library system of school libraries and where their town or district is without a children's room or even a regularly-open public library, are in the most difficult case. Sometimes the education authority allows the requisitioning of books for general reading, but there is rarely a proper fund for them, and as Mr. Evan T. Davis, the Secretary of Education for West Sussex has remarked, "almost inevitably the second, if not the first, item of expenditure attacked in an economy campaign is 'Books and Stationery.' "[1] The teachers have sometimes done remarkably well in the circumstances. By the organizing of entertainments, appeals for gifts, and other means, in some schools quite good collections have been got together. These efforts are commendable, but we hope that they may soon give way to properly organized and financed libraries.

5

What is possible in the matter may best be seen by a study of the conditions in America, where, with few qualifications, it may be said that the authorities

[1] *Library Association Record:* Supplement, 1929, p. 51.

have faith in libraries. To attempt to describe the systems in the elementary and high school and college libraries there would be beyond my powers and would trespass on the field of some admirable books to which I can refer. Those by King, Logasa, Wilson and Hutchins show to what an extent libraries in schools claim attention. I would add that every teacher should be on good terms with the public librarian, who, if he is a sensible man, will welcome inquiries as to the management of libraries.

SCHOOL LIBRARIES—GENERAL

AUTHORITIES

AMERICAN LIBRARY ASSOCIATION. School Library Year Book, No. 1. 1928—and yearly. Chicago: A.L.A.
—— Standard Library Organization and Equipment for Secondary Schools. 1928. Chicago: A.L.A.
BOARD OF EDUCATION. Report of the Consultative Committee on Books in Public Elementary Schools. 1928. Stationery Office.
—— Memorandum on Libraries in State-Aided Secondary Schools in England. 25 pp. 1928. Stationery Office.
CANT, MONICA, and Others. Public and Secondary School Libraries: four papers. 32 pp. 1929. Library Association.
FAY, LUCY E., and EATON, ANNIE T. Instruction in the Use of Books and Libraries. 1915. Boston Book Co.
FEGAN, ETHEL. School Libraries: practical hints on management. 1928. Cambridge: Heffer.
HUTCHINS, MARGARET, and Others. Guide to the Use of Libraries. 1928. N.Y.: Wilson Co.
JAST, L. STANLEY. The Provision of Books for Children in Elementary Schools. 1928. Libraco.
LOGASA, HANNAH. The High School Library: its function in education. 1928. N.Y.: Appleton.
WILSON, MARTHA. Selected Articles on School Library Experience. 1928. N.Y.: Wilson Co.

CHAPTER XIX

SCHOOL LIBRARIES: MUNICIPAL

1

An organized library service for a town would provide at each of the public libraries a children's room, with reference, lending and periodicals sections, and in every school under the local authority an individual library; and all of these would be under the supervision of the public librarian. Similarly in counties, there would be a central library in the county centre and collections in each of the schools in the towns and villages; all under supervision of the county librarian. This modern method of providing school libraries, so far as Great Britain is concerned, was initiated by Sir John Ballinger when he was librarian of Cardiff in 1898, although in some towns small collections, charged at intervals, had been lent by public libraries to schools before that; and any student of the now widespread county library system may see that it is the Cardiff system applied to villages.

2

The cardinal point about the Cardiff system is that it is a co-operation between school and library

SCHOOL LIBRARIES—MUNICIPAL

committees. The Education Committee provides the money for books and apparatus, and the library provides the service of book-selection, cataloguing, repairing and managing the circulation. The controlling body is a joint committee, consisting of four representatives of each of the two committees mentioned and two teachers chosen by the Teachers' Association. This committee met monthly at Cardiff, and considered the reports and recommendations of the librarian. I have had personal experience of a similar committee and find that it works fairly well, although there is sometimes a tendency to friction between the committees involved. At Cardiff this seems to have been absent; but I think as a general policy that the Education Committee should hand an agreed sum yearly to the Library Committee in return for an adequate library service and not receive reports other than annual ones. As a rule now, the joint committee reports to the Education Committee, which sometimes exercises its power of revision, usually in the direction of refusing to buy what it supposes to be expensive books. One education committee once laid down the rule that no book which cost more than two shillings was to be bought. That was in pre-war days, but any such rule will soon ruin a whole service. I mention these matters as the librarian must occasionally meet them: with patience and with wisdom, I hope; but several towns now work the Cardiff plan successfully.

3

The cost of the service was originally 6d. per child, but that should now be revised, and the annual grant for library purposes should not be less than £5 for each 100 children in average attendance. As a rule, in the early stages of the scheme, the library service is confined to standards four and upwards in elementary schools. At Cardiff there was a separate library for every boys' and girls' department, allowing rather more than one book for every child in average attendance above standard three; a library for the higher grade school with one book for every scholar; a library for the pupil teachers' centre of as good a character as the funds permit, and this began with about three books per student; and a service of books in embossed type for the school for the blind. All these were lending libraries. In each of the schools for the deaf, and for defective children, and in every infants' department was a collection of picture books, and stories and nature books suitable to the attainments of the pupils. This, be it remarked, was a beginning only, the intention being gradually to extend the service downwards in the elementary schools to every child in attendance.

4

Each school is provided with a locking cupboard, which, of course, may be replaced by shelves covered with a locking grill or doors, for storing the books. In later schools bookcases are provided in the

SCHOOL LIBRARIES—MUNICIPAL

building contract. A list of books is made by the librarian after inviting suggestions from all teachers in the system. This invitation may not produce many suggestions, but the teachers should always feel that their co-operation is a welcome thing. The list is then submitted to the joint committee. The first problem is the allocation of the books. As a basic stock every school should receive, or expect to receive within a period of three years, the classics of child literature such as are listed in Chapter II. Then the schools should be arranged in groups according to the number of children attending, as in the grading system now in vogue for head teacher's salaries; in such a way that in each grade there is a sufficient and representative stock in the schools collectively. The plan is that each school within the group is to receive a library and that that library shall be changed over at least once yearly for some other library in the group. This is done until the libraries reach a certain size—say 250 volumes—when they become stationary and are refreshed with additions and weeded out at regular intervals. Books travel to the schools in boxes or baskets. The venesta boxes used in some county libraries do very well. In towns or counties where a library motor service exists this matter of exchange is simple enough.

5

The overhaul and exchange of libraries is best done during the long vacation. Experience shows that this gives least inconvenience to school and, curious as it may seem to people who think children will want books in holidays more than in school session, to reader. The library staff must often be reinforced at this time, as in a fairly large town the number of books to be sent to the binders, and to be repaired, weeded out and checked is very great.

6

I have refrained from giving an annual budget of school library expenditure. It must differ considerably in a town and in a county, because the cost of transport is so much greater in the latter. A rough calculation, based on my own observations, would indicate that about 60 per cent. of the income should go on books, 20 per cent. to 30 per cent. on binding, and the balance on other charges. I am assuming that the Libraries Committee provides the service; and this work involves the whole time of a skilled assistant in a town which has more than thirty school departments, in addition to extra services during the change-over and stock-taking month.

7

There is usually a central catalogue at the public library or county centre of all the books in the libraries, which is in such form as to indicate in what schools they are placed. This is done in various ways, but I prefer the standard card (5 inches by 3 inches)

SCHOOL LIBRARIES—MUNICIPAL

with the entry at the top and the remainder of the front and the back of the card ruled with numbered squares. The cards can be printed ready for use. Each library has a number and the whereabouts of the book is shown by ringing round the numbers

Hudson, W. H.										
Afoot in England.										
301 546 822 1179							Dent 6s. 0d.			
1	2	3	4	5	6	7	8	9	10
11	12	13	14	15	16	17	18	19	20
21	22	23	24	25	26	27	28	29	30
31	32	33	34	35	36	37	38	39	40
41	42	43	44	45	46	47	48	49	50
51	52	53	54	55	56	57	58	59	60

FRONT OF CENTRAL CATALOGUE CARD; THE SQUARES ARE CONTINUED ON THE BACK

of the libraries holding it. When a change is made the numbers can be crossed through.

Each school will have a typed sheet catalogue of its own library and copies of these catalogues, filed alphabetically under the names of the schools, will serve as a record at the central library.

8

Usually the books are distributed to the children by someone appointed by the Head Teacher, who may be a senior scholar; and regular days and hours are fixed for the issue of books. There are several methods of charging, but ordinary card-charging, as described in Chapter VIII, is as good as any. Of course all the work of book accession, labelling and card-writing is done at the central library. The only label the school librarian is called upon to handle is the date label, which must be replaced when filled. There will be required in each school a supply of borrowers' cards and date labels, date stamps, ink-pads, and charging trays. The library staff will instruct the school librarian in the simple work of charging and advise him on such matters as when a book ought to be withdrawn for repair or binding and what to do to meet special demands, or such emergencies as an epidemic.

9

The rules governing the issue and return of books should be simple. These are sufficient:—

Books are lent and may be returned once (twice) a week on a regular day (or days) to be fixed by the Head Teacher.

Books may not be kept longer than fourteen days, at the end of which period the loan may if desired be renewed at the discretion of the school librarian.

Books must be kept clean and used carefully. Any imperfection, or any damage done to or found in them must be

SCHOOL LIBRARIES—MUNICIPAL

reported when the book is returned to the school librarian. The school librarian may withhold books from any scholar for neglect of the rules.

It is found that the authority of the teacher is usually sufficient to assure the proper care and punctual return of the books. When, however, a book is wilfully injured, or lost through the proved carelessness of the borrower, the head teacher should be asked to endeavour to recover its value from the parents. This will cause the parents to exercise some control over the child's treatment of the books. In some cases it will be undesirable or even impossible to press this rule, and a small amount every year must be allowed for book losses.

10

Great care should be exercised in the case of books borrowed from homes where they may have been in contact with infectious disease. The ideal would be to destroy the books, but if this is not possible the sanitary authorities should take charge of them, and disinfect them before re-circulation; and no book should go into a home that has been infected until it is certified as free from infection.

11

Periodical visits to schools should be made by the library staff who will maintain that liaison between the central library and the school which is necessary. The following are cards which can be sent monthly

A MANUAL OF CHILDREN'S LIBRARIES

from the school to the central library: of course the library supplies them for the purpose. The first is the monthly record card:—

Front of Monthly Returns Card

The Chief Librarian,
Central Library,
Northfield.

Supplies wanted
Book pockets_____
Vouchers_____
Borrowers' cards_____
Repairs put aside for treatment_____
Remarks:—
Signed_____

SCHOOL LIBRARIES—MUNICIPAL

	.... SCHOOL LIBRARY									
	Issues for the Month of .... 19—									
	0	1	2	3	4	5	6	7	8	9	Total
1st week											
2nd week											
3rd week											
4th week											
5th week											
Number of Borrowers											

Back of Monthly Returns Card

A MANUAL OF CHILDREN'S LIBRARIES

The school librarian will take stock at the annual change-over as a preliminary to the final check by the library staff; for this a good form is:—

> ———— SCHOOL LIBRARY
>
> ———— 19—
>
> The Chief Librarian,
> Central Library,
> Northfield.
>
> I have checked each book in this library with the corresponding book cards, and certify that the volumes sent to me, viz. ———— are complete with the exception of those named over.
>
> I have laid aside ———— vols. as worn out, imperfect or needing repair.
>
> ————————
> *School Librarian*
>
> FRONT OF STOCK-TAKING CARD

SCHOOL LIBRARIES—MUNICIPAL

Number	Author	Brief Title					Remarks[1]

[1] Use this column for explanations why missing, using following abbreviations:—*l* = lost; *r* = returned to Central Library for repair; *s* = sent to Sanitary Department; *m* = missing and not accounted for.

BACK OF STOCK-TAKING CARD

A MANUAL OF CHILDREN'S LIBRARIES

I have refrained from dwelling upon the incidental uses of such a library in lessons in school; these are obvious to any reader of this book. There should be constantly an exchange of ideas and opinions between school and library; and every school should have a stock of vouchers or (better still) actual borrowers' cards for use at the public library, which it hands to school leavers in order that they may continue their library career when school days are over.

AUTHORITIES

BALLINGER, JOHN. Children and Public Libraries. In British Library Year Book. 1900–01. Scott, Greenwood & Co.

BROWN, J. D. Manual of Library Economy. Chap. 33—The Library and the School. 1931. Grafton.

CARDIFF PUBLIC LIBRARIES. Cardiff School Libraries: a note on their establishment and organization. 1903.

CARDIFF EDUCATION COMMITTEE. Schools and Libraries: a note on School and Library Work, together with the Annual Report of the Librarian on the School Libraries, 1928–29.

EPILOGUE
A WORD WITH THE CHILDREN'S LIBRARIAN

CHAPTER XX

A WORD WITH THE CHILDREN'S LIBRARIAN

I

I have run briefly over a day's work in the life of a children's librarian in an earlier chapter; but I should like before closing this book to speak more definitely to those who think of making a special study of this branch of librarianship. The first qualifications for a library career are a liking for books and a liking for people. The love of books alone will not do. The would-be children's librarian should ask herself if she is able physically to stand the strain of the work; the awkward hours and the sacrifices they imply, the irritating demands and doings occasionally of children, and to give herself wholly to a service which although it has hours of pleasant occupation has also hours of severe routine not without monotony.

To be a children's librarian the love of children alone will not do. As I have said sufficiently, the problem is discipline. Can you manage children firmly and without estranging them? Have you had any experience in school or in social centres, playrooms or Sunday schools that leads you to believe that you can? It may be learnt by some people; others never acquire the power and the latter should leave this work alone.

2

An ordinary library training is essential. To be a successful librarian you must be a good book-selector, and that implies that your knowledge of literature is adequate and that you are keen to keep in touch with all its movements and its enduring books; that you are a good classifier and cataloguer, and understand library equipment and the mechanical and routine processes involved in every day's work. I prefer, as junior library assistants, people who have an interest in social service, have done some such work as teaching in Sunday school, and who like to be amongst people, and yet are book-lovers without being merely bookish. If a girl has had a Froebel training or other trained teaching experience, she is so much the better for it; but children's library work is not a refuge for those who because of broken nerves or other defect have failed as teachers. It is only fair to say that.

3

And when you are appointed, you must remember that every influence working upon child life is of importance to you. In every town there are welfare committees, girl guides, boy scouts, clubs of all kinds which are active amongst the young; you must know of them and their doings. Any conference that touches education or youth is your business. In short, you must keep in touch with all the forces that touch children; their interests must be yours.

A WORD WITH CHILDREN'S LIBRARIAN

4

The training of the Library Association or of the University of London School of Librarianship is the best you can obtain at present. If you have not obtained the diploma of one of these it should be your ambition to get it. This will make life no easy matter for you for a few years, but it is a necessary course for you to pursue if you are to keep your position in these competitive days. It is becoming more the practice than was the case formerly to appoint assistants after training at the School of Librarianship. The ultimate saving of time and of health to the person who begins library work with all the principal examinations overcome is so obvious that there is much to be said for this practice when children's librarians are involved. At present the salaries are much too low, but it is well not to enter the work if you are to spend your life in self-pity over your ill-paid state in comparison with other intellectual workers. We hope the low pay is only a stage and that things will improve, but this will depend in some measure upon *your* contribution towards making library service desirable, even indispensable to the community.

5

Once upon a time the library life could be recommended to those who liked a genteel and comfortably lazy career. So I am told, though it has not been so in my own lifetime. Now-a-days the life is strenuous, and it is not superfluous to say: look after your health and get into the open for some hours every day. In a general summary of things to be desired I would say:—Keep in touch with the world, with children, with all the other libraries that you can, join the Library Association and attend its meetings to talk with other librarians, read the library journals, especially watching those of America and other countries. Clear your mind of libraries altogether at least one day a week. I may conclude with the final paragraph from the first writing I made on this subject:—

"The work is full of interest and charm. The daily association with good books, the variety and manifold phases of character exhibited by the children, the privilege of directing their minds in their most impressionable years, of amusing, instructing, benefiting them—these are compensations for much necessary drudgery and many disheartening features. In fine, the children's librarian has a mission and a work which must appeal to all who care for children, and these comprehend the better part of mankind."

A WORD WITH CHILDREN'S LIBRARIAN

AUTHORITIES

Training: General

LIBRARY ASSOCIATION. Syllabus of the Professional Examination: together with information on facilities for study and training. 1931.

PLUMMER, MARY W., and WALTER F. K. Training for Librarianship. 1923. Chapter XIII of *A.L.A. Manual of Library Economy*. Chicago: A.L.A.

UNIVERSITY COLLEGE, UNIVERSITY OF LONDON. Prospectus of the School of Librarianship (Annually).

WILLIAMSON, CHARLES C. Training for Library Service. 1923. N.Y.: Carnegie Corporation.

Training: Special

MARTIN, HELEN. Children's Librarianship as a Profession. 18 pp. School of Library Science, Western Reserve Univ., Cleveland, U.S.A.

POWELL, SOPHY H. The Children's Library. Chap. IX—The Children's Librarian and Her Training 1917. N.Y.: Wilson Co.

Reference should be made to library journals, and many of the text-books already cited in the lists of authorities after each chapter deal with training. In America there are special Library school courses in children's work, and there is a Children Librarians' Section of the American Library Association with about 800 members, and the *Children's Library Year Book* of the A.L.A. (mentioned in the last chapter) is invaluable. In England a School Library Section of the Library Association is contemplated.

APPENDIX

SOME EXAMINATION QUESTIONS[1]

A

THE LIBRARY ASSOCIATION

B

UNIVERSITY OF LONDON DIPLOMA IN LIBRARIANSHIP
(School of Librarianship)

---

[1] *Reprinted by kind permission of the Library Association and of the University and the College, respectively. The "Year Book" of the Library Association contains all the questions set at its Examinations during the previous year, 5s. net (2s. 6d. to Members of the Association only).*

A

The Library Association

Make a list of ten ready-reference books for a children's room.

Give a brief outline of a talk to children on the care of books.

Write a brief outline story (for use with children) of "The Life of a Library Book."

Compare the position of library work with children in this country and in the United States.

Draw a rough plan of your ideal children's library, to serve possibly 5,000 users once a fortnight; give measurements in figures. Indicate the general relation of the room to other departments on the same floor, and state the accommodation for books, periodicals, staff, and users.

Detail the essentials of a well-equipped children's room.

In some libraries a department serves a double purpose (i.e. a room may be both a children's library and lecture room). What special furniture and fittings are necessary to ensure such possible use of a particular department?

Give an account, with measurements, of the necessary furniture of a modern children's room which is used as a combined lending library and periodicals room.

Draw a plan showing how a combined adult and junior lending department, with one staff enclosure for both, can be most satisfactorily arranged.

A MANUAL OF CHILDREN'S LIBRARIES

Do you consider that a junior library consisting of one room for reference, lending, and periodicals is the best medium for work with children? Discuss this, giving possible alternatives.

What form of catalogue would you provide in a children's library, and why?

What rules and regulations do you consider necessary for a children's library?

Assuming it to be necessary to limit the issue of books to children, what plan would you recommend for effecting this?

What measures are employed to avoid overcrowding in popular children's departments?

Should there be an age-limit below which it is inadvisable to admit children to public libraries?

Discuss the question of allowing children to take part in the work of the junior library as "helpers."

As it is now a common practice to receive classes of children at the library, give a brief description of the method you would adopt to explain the contents of the library. . . . Add a short letter of invitation to the head teachers.

A children's librarian is asked to give a talk to an upper class in an elementary school. Give a summary outline of what she should say.

Discuss the value of the "story hour" as an aid to work with children.

What is the value of a picture collection, and how would you set about starting one?

APPENDIX

How would you organize a children's reading circle?

It is said that a gap exists between the junior library and the adult home-reading library. How would you bridge this gap?

Do you consider that a lending library for children and another for adults satisfactorily caters for all borrowers? Should any special provision be made for young people between the ages of fourteen and seventeen, and, if so, what?

What steps would you take to ensure that children about to leave school had the claims of the adult library put before them?

It is intended to circulate a letter to all children when they leave school concerning the value to them of the public library. Indicate briefly the essential points for such a communication.

In what ways can the Education Authority usefully co-operate in the management of a junior library?

In what ways can the library department assist the elementary schools? Are there any legal powers of co-operation between them?

Outline a report to a Director of Education on a proposal to establish a school library in a central school, giving your recommendation for staff, furniture, fittings, equipment, and proportion of stock to number of scholars.

A librarian has been asked to give a series of six lectures to teachers on "Libraries and Schools." Give a list of the six divisions of the subject, summarizing each one in brief.

Compare the relative merits of a junior library at the local public library and a system of school libraries.

A MANUAL OF CHILDREN'S LIBRARIES

Books for school libraries may be circulated in batches from the library, or permanent collections may be maintained at the schools. Discuss the two methods of working and their respective merits.

State the qualifications and training desirable for a children's librarian.

Draw up a syllabus for adoption in a training school for children's librarians.

B

University of London Diploma in Librarianship
(*School of Librarianship*)

Discuss the question of "live" stock, from the point of view of a children's library, an adult lending library, and a reference library.

What instructions would you give in regard to the dimensions, materials, and any other necessary details for windows, shelving, gangways, tables, and chairs in (*a*) a lending department, (*b*) a reference department, and (*c*) a children's department in an open-access library.

Draw up a specification for tables and shelving for (*a*) a combined newspaper and reading room (70 ft. by 36 ft.), (*b*) a children's library (55 ft. by 30 ft.), and (*c*) an open-access reference library.

You are instructed to examine and report on the condition and general efficiency of *either* the lending department or the children's department of a public library. To what particular points would you direct attention?

What periodicals would you recommend for a children's reading room? Give the titles of twelve, and state whether suitable for boys or girls.

What means do librarians use to attract and maintain the interest of children?

INDEX

Access, 119
Accession, 63–73
Admission of readers, 171
Adolescents, 224, 227–228
Adult library, Relations with, 227–228
Ages of children, and reading, 36–37, 50–51
American children's libraries, 101–102
Author numbers, 139

Babees Book, 25
Ballinger, Sir J., 103, 238
Battledore, 23
Berquin, 30
Binders' tools, 81
Binding, 85, 87–93
   materials, 92–93
   publishers', 61
   sheet, 90
   slip, 91
Birkenhead, Children's work at, 100
"Blood," see "Penny dreadful"
"Blurbs," 78
Board of Education—
   Libraries in State-aided Secondary Schools, 233
   Report on Books in Elementary Schools, 58, 59, 230
Book—
   illustration, 58
   labels, 76–78
   plates, 76
   prices, 66
Bookbinding, see Binding
Bookcases, 115

Book selection, 48
   guides to, 71
Books—
   care of, 74
   orders of, 67
   physical qualities of, 38, 55–62
Bootle, School libraries, 102
British Association, *Report on School Books and Eyesight*, 57
Bunyan, John—
   Book for Boys and Girls, 27
   Pilgrim's Progress, 21, 27

Cannons, H. G. T., *Bibliography of Library Economy*, 11
Cardiff School libraries, 103, 238–241
Carroll, Lewis—
   Alice, 32, 45
   as good book-making, 35
Catalogues, 148–161
   Author entries, 148–152
   Card, 156–159
   Classified, 154
   Dictionary, 153
   School libraries, 242–243
   Sheaf, 156
Chap-books, 25
Charging system, 121
   School libraries, 244
Child-reading, Psychology of, 38–54
Children's books, Criticism of, 34–54
   History of, 22–23
Children's library, History of, 97–105

Children, Little, Books for, 43
Chivers, Cedric, 79
Christmas story festival, 178
Cinematograph, 199
Classification, 125–147
  a lesson in, 187–191
  Dewey, 126–138
  guides, 140–146
Clubs, 213–217
Collation, 74
Cost of books, 66
Cost of school libraries, 240, 242
Cribs, Book-, 65
Croydon Children's Library, 105, *et passim*
Cutting book leaves, 75

D'Aulnoy, Madame, 30
Darton, Harvey, 22, 34
Date label, 78
Day, Thomas, 30
Decoration of library, 106
Discipline, 178
"Doubtful" books, 50
Dramatic clubs, 214–216
Dramatic readings, 214

Edgeworth, Maria, 30
Education Committees and libraries, 235, 238–239
Epidiascope, 198
Equipment, 112–124
Exhibitions, 218–222
Eyesight and print, 58

Fairy story, 30, 32, 39
Floors, 120
Folk-tales, 23
Foreign books, 66
Furniture, 107, 112–124

Girls' reading, 49
Goldsmith, Oliver, 30
Gramophone, 201
Guides to card catalogue, 158
Guides to shelves, 144–146

Heating, 114
Homework, 176
Horn-books, 23
"Horrible," *see* "Penny dreadful"
Humour, Child's sense of, 47
Hunslet Junior Library, 123

Illustration collections, 219–222
  use of, 227
Imagination, Child's, 39, 46
Infectious disease, 175, 245
Injuries, 113
Insurance, 113
Islington Children's Library, 104

Jackets, 78
Janeway, James, 28
Jast, L. S., cited, 107

Keys to text books, 65

Labels, 76
Lantern, screen, 118
  slides, 197–199
Lavatory accommodation, 120
Lecture room, 118
  equipment, 192
Lecturers, 193–195
Lectures, 192–206
  arrangement of, 199–201
  connexion with books, 205
  illustrated, 197–198
  subjects, 195–197

INDEX

Librarians, Children's, 165–179, 253–257
  as lecturers, 202
  hours, 166
  salaries, 167
  training, 168
Library Association—
  Report on Durability of Paper, 57
  Resolution on children's libraries, 9, 181
Library lessons, 180–191
Lighting, 113
Lilliputian Magazine, 30
London School Board libraries, 99

Macaulay, cited, 21
Manchester, Early children's room, 100
  Young people's rooms, 107–109

Newberry, John, 29
Non-fiction, 51
Nottingham, Children's lending library at, 100
Nursery rhymes, 23

Object lessons, 185–191
Opening new books, 79
Ordering, Book, 67

Papers, Book, 55–56
Paradise Lost, 21
Parent and librarian, 225
"Penny dreadful," 31, 40–43, 45
Perrault, 30
Pictures in library, 106, 116
Pious books, 27–29

Plans, 109–111
Powell, S. H., *The Children's Library*, 11
Print, Effect of, on the eyes, 58
Printing types, 57–60
Publications, Library, 226
Publicity, 223–229
Publishers, 66

Readers, Admission of, 171–175
Reading, Influence on children, 1
  methods of encouraging, 181
Readings, 213–217
Rees, Gwendolen, *Libraries for Children*, 11, 97
"Religious" books, 27–29
Religious Tract Society, 97–98
Repairing outfits, 81
Rhodes, Hugh, *Boke of Nurture*, 25
Rules, 173–175
  School libraries, 244–245
Ruskin, John, cited, 51

Sandford and Merton, 30
School libraries, 230–250
  Municipal, 238–250
Scott, Sir W., *Ivanhoe*, 31
Screens, Illustration, 116
Shelf register, 159–161
Shelves, 115
Sherwood, Mrs., 30
Stains in books, 74
Stamping books, 75
Stationery, 121
Stock, 63–73
  book, 69
Stock-taking, School libraries, 248–249
Story Hour, 24, 176, 207–212

269

Story-telling, Training in, 210
Subject index, 142
Suggestions, Book, 65
   slips, 67
Sunday school libraries, 98–99

Talks, *see* Lectures
Teachers and librarian, 224
Thackeray, W. M., cited, 24
Tiger Tim's Weekly, 43–44

Training of librarians, 166, 253–257
Trimmer, Mrs., 30

Ventilation, 114
Vouchers, 172

Walls, Treatment of, 115
Willton, Gladys, quoted, 50
Women as librarians, 165

For Product Safety Concerns and Information please contact our EU
representative GPSR@taylorandfrancis.com
Taylor & Francis Verlag GmbH, Kaufingerstraße 24, 80331 München, Germany

www.ingramcontent.com/pod-product-compliance
Lightning Source LLC
Chambersburg PA
CBHW052219300426
44115CB00011B/1749